Stairs and Whispers:
D/deaf and Disabled Poets Write Back

Stairs and Whispers:
D/deaf and Disabled
Poets Write Back

Edited by Sandra Alland, Khairani Barokka
and Daniel Sluman

Nine
Arches
Press

Stairs and Whispers: D/deaf and Disabled Poets Write Back
Edited by Sandra Alland, Khairani Barokka and Daniel Sluman

ISBN: 978-1-911027-19-5

First published May 2017 by:

Nine Arches Press
PO Box 6269
Rugby
CV21 9NL
United Kingdom

www.ninearchespress.com

Printed in the United Kingdom by:
Imprint Digital
digital.imprint.co.uk

Nine Arches Press is supported using public funding by the National Lottery through Arts Council England.

Supported using public funding by
ARTS COUNCIL
ENGLAND

CONTENTS

7

Maps

Dreams

Legends

Access Information

🔊 bit.ly/saw1access

Audio:

Many of the poets in the anthology have kindly provided audio recordings of themselves reading their poems or essays. These, and recordings of access information, can be accessed online at Nine Arches Press' Soundcloud address: https://soundcloud.com/ninearchespress. Relevant pieces of writing are marked with this symbol 🔊 which is clickable in our e-book version, and goes directly to individual poems or essays.

Video:

Sandra Alland has curated and co-created a selection of film-poems that showcase poetry in British Sign Language and other poetry on film. In the book, film-poems are represented by a still image from each film-poem, with a URL (web address) listed beneath it; these are clickable in the e-book. All films have captions, some feature BSL, and text/transcripts of the poems appear on YouTube (in some cases these are downloadable). Some silent films also have voice-over video versions and/or Soundcloud links with audio recordings of the poems. In *Stairs and Whispers*, the poems are marked with these symbols:

Film symbol   BSL symbol   captioning symbol   audio symbol

Descriptive Text of Still Photos and Vispo (Visual Poetry):

For the cover, still photographs from film-poems, and poetry that is visual in nature (as opposed to text-based), we have provided descriptive text. Works with such text will bear the symbol:

(clickable in the e-book version) and are at the back of the book, beginning on page 225. There is an audio version of these descriptions.

Content Notes:

We've done our best to try to list topics some people may wish to avoid or know about before reading. These are at the back of the book, beginning on page 232.

D/deaf and Disabled Terminology:

Throughout the book, we use terms such as 'D/deaf', 'disabled', 'the social model', 'neurodiversity', etc. We have provided basic definitions of some concepts for those who might want such information. These are at the back of the book, beginning on page 238.

Biographies and Notes on the Poems:

More information on the poets and their processes is at the back of the book, beginning on page 242.

Links to all audio and video content:

In case of any links breaking or not working, you can find the main links through to all audio and video content for the *Stairs and Whispers* anthology here: bit.ly/stairsandwhispers

Introduction   *Jane Commane*

Between 2013 and 2014, conversations with two Nine Arches Press poets, Markie Burnhope and Daniel Sluman, touched upon the idea for what was initially outlined as an anthology of 'disability poetics'. My discussion with Markie had followed the *Fit to Work: Poets Against ATOS* project, and ideas about what could or should follow it, whilst the latter conversation was initiated by Daniel, who identified that there was, as yet, no UK companion anthology to the ground-breaking American anthology, *Beauty is a Verb.*

Both ideas came together in the right moment. There seemed to be a conspicuous absence in the contemporary UK poetry landscape (and in wider literary discourse). And it wasn't as if D/deaf and disabled poets weren't out there; they simply weren't being thought of, included, invited or considered. It's a theme that the poets and editors themselves will pick up on directly and far more eloquently than I can throughout this remarkable book, so I will allow readers to explore and consider this further within the pages that follow.

The idea of this anthology grew (as all good ideas should) firm and unshakeable roots; Daniel and Markie became editors, and brought on board a third editor, Sandra Alland. Although sadly Markie stepped down from editing due to health issues in 2016, we were very fortunate that Khairani Barokka was able to join the editorial team, and bring her instincts and insight to further enrich the anthology. Under the careful stewardship of its editors, *Stairs & Whispers* has grown vigorously from those early, vital seedlings of ideas that began life in conversations at a crowded book fair in London and on a chilly April morning at the Wenlock Poetry Festival.

Together, the editors refined and interrogated what the ideal anthology should be, what it should (and shouldn't) contain, who it must include, and what its terms of engagement and reference would be. The submission guidelines further made this clear – creating a manifesto for the anthology that was ambitious and deeply rooted in a politically and socially aware approach to issues that affect the everyday lives of D/deaf and disabled people.

What was clear from the outset was that the editors were determined that this would be an anthology by and for D/deaf disabled poets, which centred their voices and would be entirely directed by them. As a publisher (and non-disabled person), my contribution has been to ensure I create that space for this vital work to take place, to fund and support that work, and to ensure that the platform Nine Arches Press has as a publisher can be used to magnify and amplify the poets this book sets out to foreground.

This is especially vital in our contemporary situation, where we are witnessing the systematic dehumanisation of disabled people by the government and the state in the UK and beyond. Brutal benefits cuts and the removal of services, access and support (not to mention human rights) are brazenly coupled with deeply negative and damaging media narratives, which in turn create an atmosphere where abuse, prejudice and violence is further normalised.

Amidst this, D/deaf and disabled people are often shut out (literally and physically) and frequently spoken for, over, or about in our media and culture. Too often, their stories are taken and retold to fulfil a certain agenda. Ever more vital then, to work against this and create or open up spaces where D/deaf and disabled people can answer back – and indeed, write back – for themselves.

Dylan Thomas said that 'a good poem helps to change the shape of the universe'. I believe that a good anthology helps to change the shape of the universe too – and not just for the poets it brings together, but the communities of poetry it plays a part in defining. A good anthology also changes the shape of things to come for communities of readers now and in the years ahead; it creates new readerships, changes plans, opens doors and alters the list of possibilities. I hope that Stairs and Whispers will be instrumental in creating new poets, showing how D/deaf and disabled poets before them have wielded the power of poetry's distinct language of possibilities to give voice, space and page-room to the expression of human experiences.

From the beginning, the editors were also committed to ensuring that this project was as accessible, wide-ranging and diverse as possible. Their efforts speak for themselves – from known backgrounds and experiences, over three quarters of the writers in the anthology are women, over 20% are BAME, and more than a third are LGBTQ+. Also, it is notable that this anthology is representative geographically as a national survey, with poets spread regionally across Scotland, England, Wales and Northern Ireland.

Here, you will find a superb selection of poets writing with ferocity, brilliance, and humour. In recent months, as I've come to know the poems in this book intimately, I've frequently found myself returning to them and each time finding afresh a new phrasing or image that strikes me so clearly that it insists on me taking a little more time in its company. There are poems here that are piercingly honest, angry, consoling, and throughout a potent sense of precision that is keen to challenge and push at the boundaries. In addition, I love the fact that this anthology introduces me to new writing from a number of emerging poets alongside work from more established poets whose work I am already a little more familiar with. Though I know I am a little biased, I think readers will find some of the best and most vital examples of contemporary poets at work between these pages.

The editors' and poets' commitment to realising the full ambitions and accessibility of this book has been outstanding. Sandra Alland collated over 80 tracks of audio made by contributors, and brought together nine films (including BSL poetry). The editors also created content notes, descriptive text of images, and disabled and D/deaf definitions. In addition, they worked closely with each poet, commissioned essays, ordered the selection and put in countless hours that created this anthology's distinct and powerful reading experience. Their endeavours result in a print and eBook anthology that is broad, welcoming, and accessible in every way that has been possible.

And this is only the beginning. The roots this book has so readily put down are now breaking new ground; I hope that successive years see *Stairs and Whispers* play a vital role in bringing future D/deaf and disabled poets to the foreground, and be instrumental in the building of new platforms from which they can be read or signed, heard or seen.

It has been a privilege and pleasure to have played a small part in supporting and publishing *Stairs and Whispers.* I am enormously proud of this bold, influential and provocative book that the editors and the poets have made together. Long may its roots reach, and long may its effects be felt.

On Living Our Poetries   *Khairani Barokka*

In a world obsessed with diagnostics, numerical measurements, finite pathways to recovery, and the absolute need for such recovery in a body deemed less than able, regardless of whether or not one already feels whole, or whether our conditions have cures if we identify as sick, I would prefer to describe my disability in colours, shades and nuances. The blunt trauma of being forced into one diagnosis, then another, of having my bodily and psychic sensations dismissed, diminished, mistreated and ignored, over many years, in hospitals, clinics, schools and public spaces in various countries, has sharpened my utmost regard for the tool that is poetry. It is through stanza that communion happens between the shades of life that we all know can't be enumerated, can't be delineated, can't be kept hidden from ourselves – despite how ignorance about our varied, glorious bodies and minds perpetuates systemic violence and forced disconnection, even from our own experiences.

Lack of access to healthcare in the past means my conditions of extreme chronic pain and fatigue, and other symptoms over my chest and right side, are very much socially-imposed disablements. 'Disabled', as we all (should) know, is the opposite of 'enabled', not 'unable', and I was left unenabled, to suffer unnecessarily for years, for a number of reasons that have become clear in hindsight.

Because I was brown and a woman, because women's pain of many kinds is known to be underestimated and undertreated, because I lived in Brooklyn in an area where nearby hospitals served other brown folks, communities of colour, in circumstances that still leave me aghast in memory. Because I lived in and come from a country, Indonesia, attempting to recover from hundreds of years of colonialist resource extraction, then a dictatorship and mass murder, where neurologically-complex care and mental healthcare are precious and rarely done well. Where communities are fighting not to fray under socioenvironmental ills, and disabled girls generally don't end up this lucky – I have loved ones, and over the years they have learned that although I didn't expect my physique to feel this way years ago, I am stubborn as hell, and demand nothing less than absolute love for a body that's taken more than its share. That all of us are more than the sum of our parts. Neglect has meant I am taking longer to understand coping mechanisms, but this body is not somehow incomplete or lacking because it is internally different from an 'abled' prior state. It is showing its strength and persistence. It exists fully in the now, not in an alternate universe as 'more able'. As a relatively recent transplant to the UK, I am deeply grateful for the opportunity to recognise those in our communities as always fully present in this way, through literature, and to understand how each of us conveys differently our varied experiences here.

The situation for disabled communities in Indonesia, and other countries with less access to accessibility and healthcare resources, is infinitely worse than in the UK, but the UK has indelible complicity in this lack, as do other Western countries: countries and communities are not 'developing' but *under*developed, as a result of legacies of brutal resource transfer, slavery, governments installed by other governments to 'stabilise' and also to oppress. Within the UK, resources flow towards some and not others. Bleeding rural communities of resources breeds disablement within those communities, as does treating immigrants and refugees as criminals, denying the need for bodies and lives to be honoured, in our infinite variety, in our various likelihoods of survival, in our universal need to form community and to be treated as human. When D/deaf and disabled communities are doubted, criminalised as benefit scroungers, and simultaneously pitied, an upswell of resistance demands attention, and so too does poetry reflecting our emotions in this climate demand to be read.

It's been just over a year since I was finally prescribed medicine I should have been given at least five years before, if the innumerable healthcare providers I saw had offered a proper pathway towards holistic pain management. And before that, there were other stories I am continuing to work through, primarily in one way: throughout the years, my salvation has been the innate desire to read to and to contribute to the world of poetry in many forms, where the transformation of emotion into language and back seemed and continues to seem iridescent, a work of magic when done well. Though not all first-person poems I've written are autobiographical, nor are those of others, and not all poetry is written in first-person perspective, through it we go beyond appreciation of our inner selves, and inhabit, momentarily, other lived experiences.

Questioned as to whether my pains are real until I am in a situation where I can no longer visually 'pass' for abled, poetry is a conduit for both illumination and mystery. Through poetry, I can be both in pain and doing well (including as I write these words), an intellect and carnal, a fabulist and a memoirist, a Muslim feminist who grew up knowing that binaries are false and rarely kind in implementation – both suffering from and struggling through physical pain, and fiercely proud of being disabled, as a much-misunderstood and greatly-varied denomination.

Poetry is where I have attempted to translate between disabled and non-disabled worlds, but my work is most at home with D/deaf, disabled and crip compatriots. I'm grateful for the opportunity to have joined the editorial team of Stairs and Whispers, and it has been such an honour to be amongst these poets, in shared understanding of the liminal nature of being in a body, in shared release of exhaustive misunderstandings and hurts, slights and continual expectations of speaking on behalf of all of our kind, and also expectations of speaking in tongues the abled can relate to. This, however, is for us. To laugh and weep within, to be still and to be angry alongside. It has been such a joy to play with language with my co-editors and with these contributors, in dialogue, in solidarity, as indeed we all write back.

shove ten pounds of sugar   *Daniel Sluman*
in a seven pound bag

the poem is an artefact
made from words
& the space that exists
between & around the words

the spaces
are the negative of the words
part of a reciprocal
dialectic relationship
with the words

(without the spaces
there are no words)

*

i am human
the shape of my body
exists within space

there are gaps & absences
within & around my body
every human has a unique set
of absences created by their body

(without the absences
there is no body)

*

my absences
are perhaps more apparent
than other people's

i have an absence
where my left leg should be

as a reader / passer-by
you will notice the absence
of my left leg

the absence
will be more powerful
than if my leg was there

(shove ten pounds of sugar
in a seven-pound bag)

*

the absence forces you
to ascribe meaning to it

forces you to project
your own emotional /
intellectual self
within the absence

(mommy why has that man's leg
fallen off ?)

i am a walking signifier

*

the page is a canvas
screen
stage

the poet reflects
(disassembles)
themselves
on the page

each space is apt
each word is placed
like ice in water

as a crippled writer
you can put your body
into the poem
with all its faults
scars
gaps

they'll dry like ink
from the damp notation
of your self

*

the disabled writer
turns the page
into a mirror

reflecting the reader's
own mortality   their fears
nightmares   the *i couldn't live like that*

we are on the fine end of a wedge
we can see aspects of societal behaviour
which they may not (wish to)
see themselves

a dead russian writer once said
that all good writing
is defamiliarisation

that all good writing
will get to the heart of an object / concept

(make the stone
stony again)

& turn it into art

disability defamiliarises life
forces you to question
could i do that ?

*

bonecancer at 11
& the disarticulation of a limb
has been a blessing
i would thank in prayer
every day if i believed god
was listening because
i know all this
immediate noise & fizz
is bunk / nothing / zero
& i would not be who
i am now without
that wonderful magic trick

see   his leg *has* disappeared !

a trick so real
no one stands to applaud

🔊 bit.ly/saw2shove

Nothing About Us Without Us, No One Left Behind

Sandra Alland

> *Writing *to* disabled people has all sorts of implications, not just topic and diction but orientation, the things you don't explain but just let float out there. When I consciously undertook writing poems with a crip audience in mind, I let go of the myth of universality.*
> — Jim Ferris, *Poetry* magazine, 2014

> *We cannot comprehend ableism without grasping its interrelations with heteropatriarchy, white supremacy, colonialism and capitalism. Each system benefits from extracting profits and status from the subjugated 'other'.*
> — Patty Berne, *Skin, Tooth, and Bone – The Basis of Movement is Our People: A Disability Justice Primer*, Sins Invalid, 2016

Writing *to* Disabled, Crip and/or D/deaf Communities

In 2014, I was approached by Markie Burnhope, Daniel Sluman and Nine Arches editor, Jane Commane, to be co-editor of an anthology of disabled and D/deaf poets. Markie, Daniel and I began a beautiful conversation about what it means to be a disabled writer, and what disability poetics is and isn't, and hasn't yet become. Sadly, Markie left the editorial team because of health issues, but she has remained a vital part of the project. In 2016, Daniel and I continued and reshaped our conversations with a brilliant new co-editor, Khairani Barokka. Together we three selected poems and moulded them into a book.

From the get-go it was clear that many non-disabled people would immediately frame 'disability' as something specific in their minds, and that even some disabled people might have internalised non-disabled and hearing ideas about disabled and D/deaf identities, experiences, cultures – and poetry.

We made it clear in our call-out that the book was not for writing *about* our communities, but writing *by* our communities.

The non-disabled people who objected to this and wanted to be published were few, but yes, it happened, and yes, those people felt entitled to proclaim their right to our spaces and stories. Dismantling ableism and privilege is a long process indeed.

In the call-out, written by Markie, Daniel and me, we attempted to define disability as broadly as possible, not based on narrow assumptions and medicalised notions of 'impairment', and moving towards intersectional ideas of disability justice in a UK[1] framework:

We plan to draw on the context of anti-Atos/Welfare Reform and NHS privatisation activism, whose leading lights (particularly on online social networks) have been women, including trans women, queer women and/or women of colour – a clear antithesis to the systemic norm. In both poetry and prose we plan to explore, creatively and critically, other bodily identities and oppressions that intersect with disability to create what poet and activist Eli Clare called 'marked bodies'. Racialised bodies, gender non-conforming bodies, bodies 'marked' by class or religion.

As editors we are committed to the social model of disability (with contributions from other radical socio-political models), which means we are casting a wide net in our call for poets who self-identify as disabled, people with disabilities, crip, D/deaf, or any variation thereof, and who may consider their impairments and/or their disabled or D/deaf identity a key part of their thematic, conceptual and aesthetic practice... We also aim to include D/deaf writers/performers who do not identify as disabled...

I was over the moon at the possibility of helping bring into the (UK) world something as important as a collected work by disabled and D/deaf poets; in fact it made me a bit weepy. Why? Because I know thousands of brilliant, innovative and talented disabled, D/deaf and/

---

[1]   I use this term as shorthand for Wales, Scotland, Northern Ireland and England, but I in no way subscribe to the unification it suggests nor the empire this 'country' exerts.

or crip writers, artists, filmmakers, musicians and performers – but most non-disabled people would struggle to name one of them.

At this moment in time (and place), writers and performers from our communities are particularly absent from the main stage. The primary reason is the same old reason, and overlaps with the reasons all marginalised people are absent – people who are trans, gender diverse, black, racialised, queer, working class and/or from other marginalised groups are all familiar with being left out of the publishing, performance and promotion of literature. It's plain old oppression in a white supremacist, classist, heterosexist, cissexist, (trans)misogynist and ableist world.

Non-disabled people are generally not interested in our stories, unless of course they're telling them. Unless our bodies and minds are performing the struggle of the noble, pitiable crip, or the deformed villain whose evil manifests itself in disability, or the supercrip who overcomes their disability to attain a place in the 'normal' world (often by engaging in a cis/hetero- and romance-normative relationship). Unless we act as foils for the development of a non-disabled character. Unless we are so very grateful.

And sometimes, unless we are otherwise acceptable as white and middle class.

Our absence as disabled and D/deaf people in some ways also has to do with writing communities in the United Kingdom being arguably somewhat behind the United States[2] in terms of organising around disability poetics. And it has to do with the recent prominence of a specific kind of spoken word and performance poetry – and a neoliberal and capitalist focus on writers being slick and attractive packages who will sell books on tour.

If you search online about how to submit a manuscript to publishers or agents, you'll find that even smaller and independent publishers are now citing the ability to tour and read your work aloud (and they mean *with flair*) as requirements of submitting a book.

---

[2]   I use this term as shorthand for one part of the occupied and unceded territories of the many indigenous nations of Turtle Island that settlers refer to as several single 'countries', including the United States, Canada and Mexico.

This ableist idea of 'writing' is now embedded in publishing because it's also embedded in funding, controlled by arts councils, charities and others who experience (and sometimes exert) more and more pressure to promote neoliberal tourism and agendas for international trade and profit.

Difficulties in finding publishers and performance opportunities are multiplied for disabled or D/deaf poets who are, for example, also indigenous, Muslim, intersex, non-binary, bisexual, subjected to fattism or sizeism, older, working poor and/or migrants and asylum seekers not from white-majority English-speaking colonies and ex-colonies. Part of the promotion of 'good literature' at home and abroad depends on tropes of the UK being a democratic, freedom-loving place, and many people from marginalised communities do not tell this story.

Writing *by* disabled and D/deaf people is foundational to this anthology, but also writing *to* – there is resistance and strength in refusing to seek the normative world's approval, in creating our own stories in our own ways, and in telling them to each other in our own spaces (whether that be in person, in print, or online). In many cases and historically, our disabled and D/deaf co-conspirators might have been the only ones listening, watching, reading or touching us. They are the ones who have given us value. They are our main concern.

When you can't even get into the room, how do you participate? And then the question eventually becomes, do you want to participate in that particular room – or do you prefer to make a new room, and let others come to you on your terms?

Access: Leave No One Behind

But let's start with that room – because, to be frank, one cannot survive on love alone, and we often need access to that room to survive.

Most poetry readings are held in inaccessible spaces; there's no step-free entrance to the building, the reading or slam is in the basement, there's no British Sign Language interpreting or captions offered, and/or there are no single and accessible gender-neutral toilets. Despite these being the most basic of access requirements, most non-disabled people who lead reading series or festivals still don't commit to providing them. As a writer seeking to be published, you're generally required to read or perform publicly – but you can't.

The barriers to disabled and D/deaf poets participating in reading and publishing go far beyond the wheelchair-accessible building. Fewer even than accessible spaces for audiences are accessible stages; it seems not to occur to most venues and organisers that a disabled person might be behind the mic. Other considerations include: freedom from loud and distracting background noise and fluorescent or flashing lights; hearing loops, speech-to-text, lip-speaking and deaf-blind interpreting; a location that can be reached by affordable and accessible public transit; and provision of large print, Braille, audio description, easy English, comfortable chairs, quiet space outside of the main reading space, a scent-free environment, and relaxed performances.

And then there's the being invited in the first place. Because the main barrier tends to be in the imagination, in the fact that most non-disabled and hearing people don't even think about reading, watching or listening to disabled and D/deaf writers. They don't imagine our existence at all, except perhaps as bad metaphors for their own work.

The spoken word scene, for example, often demands that writers do not read from the page; it's inherently ableist to assume everyone can memorise (or be anxiety-free). There's also a focus on smooth and fast talking and on meticulous time-keeping, which can exclude people with stammers or stutters, D/deaf people, people with cerebral palsy, people who speak quietly or not at all, people who shout or tic, neurodiverse people, people in mental distress, people in chronic pain or on medication, and/or mad folks. Similar barriers exist for submitting to magazines and journals: no BSL information and lack of blind-friendly websites are just two examples.

Another barrier that isn't often considered is the social barrier. Many disabled people don't or can't go out, for reasons including but not exclusive to the physical and mental inaccessibility of events. And social networking in person is one of the foundations of 'getting ahead'. If disabled and D/deaf people can't get to the party and don't drink with those in power, we are unlikely to be remembered when opportunities arise. Also, plans get made in the pubs, often the posher ones – places that are often not only inaccessible but also additionally unfriendly to disabled and D/deaf people who are racialised or BAME, trans, gender non-conforming, femme, queer, working class, non-English-speaking or non-drinking.

Even in our own communities, we often struggle. LGBT and queer communities are far behind in providing access for disabled and D/deaf LGBTQ+ people, for example, and often participate in our oppression. Leftist protests and marches about neoliberal policies that deeply affect us are often planned without thought to how we might participate or lead, and tend to further exclude disabled people who are also sex workers, people of colour and/or from disadvantaged socio-economic backgrounds.

For non-disabled, disabled, hearing and D/deaf people alike, learning about access is a continual process. The easiest way to begin this journey is to lose our defensiveness when someone highlights their exclusion. It takes time and commitment to become accessible, and it's not a goal we can ever fully attain; it's almost impossible to be accessible to all people at all times. But hopefully more and more publishers, organisers and fellow poets will begin to seriously contemplate the phrase 'leave no one behind' – and make efforts towards access, following the lead of disabled and D/deaf people in their communities.

Stairs and Whispers: One Part of an Ongoing Conversation

Okka, Daniel and I spent hundreds of hours reading and re-reading (and in my case watching) over 120 disabled and D/deaf poets who sent their work our way. It was exhausting work, especially for three disabled and chronically ill people; but more importantly it was energising work, work that felt vital and stamped itself forever into our hearts. I felt honoured to do this work, and then to edit it into the beautiful beast it has become. And I'm grateful to have spent so much time dreaming and working with two people to whom I never had to *explain*.

We could not publish everyone, and there's no way we can ever represent everyone. But in these pages and online you'll find the writing and performances of 54 outstanding and varied disabled and/or D/deaf writers, most of them women, and many of them from backgrounds and experiences not often represented in UK publishing. We present poets who explore hospitalisation, illness, state violence, colonialism, and daily microaggressions around disability, Deaf culture, race, class, gender and sexuality. Poets who examine fiction, reality, personal relationships, nature, fantasy worlds, dreams, nightmares, resistance to pathologisation and erasure. Poets and performers who experiment with form, translation, sound and visuals, who delve into Surrealism and Vispo. Brilliant poets with much to contribute to mainstream poetics, whose work should be widely read, watched, listened to and promoted.

We follow in the tradition of resistance by groups like Survivors' Poetry and others before us, and support the ongoing creative activism of collectives like Sins Invalid and Sisters of Frida – and the many others who struggle against austerity and oppression on their own, including online and in their personal lives. We hope *Stairs and Whispers: D/deaf and Disabled Poets Write Back* will contribute to more serious and deserved study of disabled and D/deaf poetics, and to the continuation of years and years of resistance and creativity from our disabled and D/deaf ancestors and colleagues.

No one left behind. Nothing about us without us. Solidarity always.

🔊 bit.ly/saw03Alland

Bodies

Equilibrium   *Kuli Kohli*

I've faced the ground in cruel environments;
hostile temperatures, earth fractured to dust
in the erosive wind, rain, sleet and snow.

My eyes fixed on the ground,
the path lit by beaming
searchlights – only predicting
the next stride or two.

Struggling through bleak slippery mud,
I avoid iced puddles, frozen solid, hoary,
hazardous glittering pavements.

I survive crossing roads, bridges,
tree roots, rocks and uneven slabs;
collecting coppers, notes, a diamond earring
on my travels; people's lost possessions.

I barely look forward or above;
all I have to lose is my balance.

Voter in Blue   *Abi Palmer*

I look forward to the day your wife's brother dies
from an infectious and largely unheard-of disease.
All coffee and cake neighbours will attain
a series of unavoidable engagements. She sits
at the kitchen table, waiting for the call from her oldest
and dearest school friend. It never comes. You wonder
why Mr. B at number 47 so pointedly refuses to catch
your eye, as you simultaneously hose mock-Tudor
brick dust off identical navy hatchbacks, and collide
on the road towards Tesco Express. Blame
goes unsaid: the brother, his wayward friends, the NHS,
the parents – a startling lack of foresight, and yet

Three months pass. Dinner does not regain
its pinch of salt. She is hunched, withdrawn,
forgetting to comb the cowlick
at the back of her head. One Sunday,
on the mottled couch you lean, to claim
your periodical embrace. Instead,
she avoids your face, stares
at the rug, gnaws flaking lips.
That's when you speak aloud:
'You know, I never asked for this.'

🔊 bit.ly/saw04voter

body language *Abi Palmer*

draw your curtains and step
onto the escalator
into a cable car. close
the doors and travel
up the mountain

there's a leather
belt around your
levi 501s – fasten
the buckle. the hot
iron is hanging just
above your waist

you're a house. close
the downstairs windows

lay on your front,
there's a pin on the mat

lay on your back
and deflate
the red balloon

🔊 bit.ly/saw05body

Government Body

Abi Palmer

mutated limbs jerk spastically   slap each other out of the way and
bicker for bread   one hand will never talk to his own arm   they
argue for shirtsleeves   a valve bursts   arteries cough politely and
queue for blood   which spurts and gushes through pinpricks in
your flank   failing to stop it you cut off both your legs   we gasp
  a foot goes black   all eyes turn to fallen stockings and glare

🔊   bit.ly/saw06gov

she's punctuation she's mean green fisted stomach clenched fist
alpha female uber bitch slap she's my future wrinkles not merry
laughter lines or crow's feet but the clenched teeth and fixed frown
jowly rotten stare at the damp cracked wall of my nursing
home she's every painful rap against my arthritic knuckles she's the
walking cane the early bitter middle age she's salt she's lime she's
ulcers she's the pool of rancid spit from constant grinding
nightmares haunted dreams of all the things I saw somebody else
achieve she's all the things I know that I will never no she's not the
drive that makes me who I am she's the choke that stops me short
and wants to throw away the driver's key to sit and stop and watch
the traffic and there's always someone else driving ahead of me on
the one hand they're a road to follow on the other well I hope they crash

🔊 bit.ly/saw07shes

Abigail has suffered injury to the left side of her corpus striatum. It is possible that this injury occurred at some time around delivery. It is not however clear that earlier delivery would have avoided this.

5   Delivery of Abigail's head was more difficult than is often the case. Her body was delivered through the uterine incision. Her mother then watched her body go blue before the consultant arrived. The consultant extended the incision in the uterus and this allowed delivery.

10   The reasons for this are explained the expert in obstetrics. One not uncommonly sees the fetus delivered by breech Caesarean section where there is difficulty with delivering the head. In very difficult circumstances, the fetus may suffer injury due to APA. In these infants however, one expects delivery in a poor condition so that resuscitation is
15   required. The infant will become unwell and need admission to the baby unit. Characteristically if injury has occurred there is a neonatal encephalopathy.

It is therefore my view prior to multidisciplinary discussion, that it is
20   unlikely that delivery without the difficulty in delivering Abigail's head, could have altered the outcome.

darkness. - relationship between play and the poems

In this case staining of caused by lucrece's powerless Loss of virginity is its own trigger into further

As father and husband stain the streets, carrying the bleeding body through Rome

Onlookers observe the 'black blood,' 'corrupted blood,' along with 'blood untainted',

 bit.ly/saw08double

 p.227

This body has not   *Claire Cunningham*

This body has not jumped in the air more than an inch or so
It has not run on a beach
It has not fired a gun
It has not ridden a camel
It has not danced a waltz
It has not dived into a swimming pool
It has not punched someone in anger
It has not given birth
It has not spat in someone's face
It has not played a football match
It has not arranged a pension
It has not ridden a surfboard
It has not carried a television
It has not gone for a jog
It has not fixed a car engine
It has not burgled someone's house
It has not been in love
It has not killed someone in a car accident
It has not played at skipping
It has not climbed a mountain
It has not been arrested
It has not painted a ceiling
It has not run away
It has not sexually assaulted someone
It has not eaten caviar
It has not carried a coffin

🔊 bit.ly/saw09thisbody

First Contact

Claire Cunningham

under a gentler hand
with heat.
with soul.
with touch that gives as it takes
as it takes.
and when i'm held in the palm of your hand
i am all there.
entire.
whole.

not broken in pieces
to be held up to the light
to be looked through

i am on file.
you have the right to read me.

🔊 bit.ly/saw10first

Poem in which I take a knife   *El Clarke*

And cut into the heart of you.
Your purple-red inner fluids
Run over my fingers – under nails stained
With evidence of the cut.

Your flesh, smooth to the outside and soft
Within, a mess of vessels and the muscular.
Your centre is hard – the knife won't go through.

I score around the edges, dividing flesh
Gently moving, a slicing prayer.

Twist, cerise liquid sprays up the arm,
As I take the flesh
And throw aside the stone.

🔊 bit.ly/saw11poeminwhich

"As someone with EDS – a diagnosis which took 15 years – I recognise on a personal level how 'invisible' many disabled people are, and how, as a group, disabled people are labelled as 'other' in multiple ways. On the level of my work, even before diagnosis, issues with my body and mind informed my poetry, with concepts of wellness, ability, and judgement featuring thematically.

Poets, storytellers and creatives of all kinds who work despite, or even because of, their disability need recognition. There needs to be understanding within the wider community that disabled does not mean incapable, and that the difficulties many face on a day-to-day basis inform considered, important, and beautiful work.

Further, as a gay woman who grew up in a disadvantaged household, I have always felt that my voice is less likely to be heard than many others. I grew up believing that writing was a dream, not a profession, and I feel that anthologies such as this could help people growing up in a similar situation to understand that their voice is important, and that their work is valid."

– El Clarke

What I Did Today   *Debjani Chatterjee*

Today I blew up the Northern General – again;
bulldozed the waiting room in Hell
where I had sat all morning in a silly gown;
I strangled the arrogant GP who knew so little
but pretended to know it all;
my itching hands throttled the oncologists:
the indifferent one who swanned off on holiday,
forgetful of referring me for a Hickman Line
under anaesthesia at a half-decent hospital,
and the one who lost my consent form and thrust me
into a nightmare place of endless screams;
I fought the boffin butcher who drilled holes in me;
and finally I exterminated
every homicidal sidekick masquerading
as an angel of mercy...
All these things and more I did today.

🔊 bit.ly/saw12whatidid

Nebuliser

Miki Byrne

A brittle ampoule is snapped.
Cracks like the crunch
of a beetle underfoot.
Pours Salbutamol, saline,
into a tube-fed chamber.
A transparent moulded mask
links to this reservoir,
shaped to cover mouth and nose.
Provide a tight seal.
A button is pressed, motor fires,
loud for its jewellery box size
(too disturbing for books or TV)
that shines white, cleanly clinical.
At odds with her bright bedroom,
soft curves of décor.
Strap fixed at the back of her head,
its umbilical draws compressed air.
Bubbles it through the chamber
to billow steam-like clouds
as drug and air mix.
Tickles like gentle drizzle,
softly dampens her upper lip.
She inhales deeply.
Hears the magnification
of her own ragged breathing,
her heart's pulse thumping
in her head.
It's the noise of it that she hates.

🔊 bit.ly/saw13nebuliser

Disabled Woman Swimming   *Miki Byrne*

She moves with aching slowness.
Goose pimples shoaled over skin,
Feet stepping tenderly upon textured tiles.
To reach the pool's edge.
She does not dive, throw herself in,
or prayer-point her hands
and cleave water like a blade.
Will not even jump, to strike the surface
like a barrel, but steps slowly
down the ladder. Backwards.
Twisted fingers tightly clutch cold steel rails.
Slip on a meniscus of water
that threatens her grip.
She shivers as water rises, chills feet,
ankles, calves inch by slow inch.
Muscles tense with anticipation.
Water creeps higher still,
until she stands waist deep.
Scoops water over shoulders, face.
Takes a breath. Holds it. Ducks.
Pushes scarred feet off the tiled wall.
Takes another breath through damaged lungs,
stretches the shoulder that was repaired
and swims.
Released from her body's own drag,
the euphoria of buoyancy lifts her.

🔊 bit.ly/saw14swimming

Registered   *Holly Magill*

There's a document somewhere certifying
me as having a bit of something but
not the whole of it: I am 'Partial'.
A half-full glass that I might smash
from your table, 'cause it's clear
I can't see it, right.
So you'd best not let me come
to your house, certainly not
in polite company.
Those are my papers:
I'm taken as read.

🔊 bit.ly/saw15registered

'Help Wanted' *Holly Magill*

He shunts me like a wrongly stacked box of Walkers crisps;
not heavy, but awkward – away from the nanas
queuing for cat food and lottery tickets;
sharp ears belie hearing aids.

In the buzz of the violet fly-light,
he bends into my face as if to kiss. Don't I see
how difficult it would be for someone like me?

My typed CV, new GCSEs pinging,
my clean, stubborn hands –
I've made this difficult for him.

As Deputy Manager, he's a duty
of care, Health and Safety considerations;
step-stools I'd topple from, rockfalls of tinned beans
teetering to the brink of high shelves to concuss me;
I might sue. Too risky, insurance,
financial implications.

He shakes his head, a kindly uncle, palms cast
helpless across his strip-lit realm: can't I see,
he's only thinking of me.

🔊 bit.ly/saw16help

'What Can You See?' *Holly Magill*

The question could be practical,
well-intentioned, but it pins
me down completely.

My answer confuses her:
'What can *you* see? '

'Er, normal, I guess…'
I shrug: 'Yeah, me too.'

🔊 bit.ly/saw17what

Vascular Graft   *Grant Tarbard*

The anaesthesiologist billows
fogs of gas as I undertake the third operation.

The surgeon bellows confidently,
'We'll make those veins stand up and take notice'.

Stabbing at my flesh, the cannula
is a slap in the face, then a touch of sleep.

My teeth and gums almost vicious with morphine,
I rest on gnawing bone in a thin-lipped sneer.

In my recovery through the windows,
the lampposts leer like sickles.

🔊 bit.ly/saw18vascular

When Under Sodium Pentothal   *Grant Tarbard*

My leg is split in two,
clamps keeping the exposed pink tendons

of the supple flesh peeled,
the shadow of my emptied skin

like slopping black conjured coat tails
exposing my nakedness,

my innards laid out on my belly.
Stand down, all light ends here

on the saccharine edge
that makes the teeth jangle.

🔊 bit.ly/saw19sodium

Kintsugi   *Abigail Penny*

Your golden arteries will shimmer,
we'll seal your scars with silver.

We'll fill the holes with rubies,
present you in the British Museum.

An ivory tusk will work as a leg,
you'll be the centrepiece at dinner parties.

Your skin's falling from the hinges.
Let's rip the Turner and Picasso,
wrap you in masterpieces.

Your eyes look good in sapphire,
they bring out the mercury in your veins.

Paper Plate Faces   *Abigail Penny*

Everywhere I see
      paper plate faces

Purple smiling
then red cross-eyed

All the faces change
sometimes all together
in a stained glass wave
my face is grey

I walk into an exhibition
      can I make green fascination?
pull together some lines
the paper faces stare back

I go into a bookstore
a face is smiling sparkles
I spill confetti,
leave without cleaning up

It is an ancient art
I was never taught;
pipe cleaners and beads
dusty in a glass jar

In my room
      I can make the wrong faces
         all my colours
mixed,
    all my lines
scribbles

Generations   *Abigail Penny*

An artist wrestles the canvas,
punches holes into its skin
till it bleeds with colour.

A musician hammers the keys,
fingers bruising rhapsodies
and teeth smashing laments.

A writer sits in her chamber,
looks out of a frozen window.
A crow calls on a mulberry branch.
She takes a pen, stabs her thigh,
and as the blood dries
forgets the song.

"Due to my anxiety around communicating verbally, I prefer to express myself through writing. Before getting into the University of Gloucestershire I spent three years at home, with no job, no friends, and no prospects. Ever since going to university I've had jobs, gone to plays, and seen places and done things I thought I was incapable of doing.

Being labelled autistic is a double-edged sword: on one hand, it can get you the help you need, especially if you're young, but as soon as you hit 18 it becomes a burden, a big sticky label on your forehead to cover up before you go into a job interview. Autism is seen as a childhood illness, and autistic adults feel the pressure of hiding their disability. What's worse, not only does the autism label change how others see you, but how you see yourself."

– Abigail Penny

Body Polish   *Jacqueline Pemberton*

I am naked on this slab,
Let's start again.
Find me buried under
More than
Half a century.
Use salt and grain
To grind away
This callus.
I want to be
Benfogleated;
Fresh-faced,
Colgate clean,
Dig beneath
The kelp and
Crustaceans,
Scoop the debris
Between my ribs,
Turn me over,
Scrub my skin
Until it's raw,
Work your way
Into my scalp,
Behind my eyes,
The trench of
My tongue,
Polish me,
Hollow me,
Watch the slurry
Swirl and whirl,
Then wrap me in
A cloak of pearl,
Leave the room
While I become
A mermaid.

Threadbare   *Raisa Kabir*

A distance impales your desire,
Leaves you numb.
Unravelling the failing seams
That were straining to contain you.
Scratching at the stitches
Embedded in the grain of your own fabric.
Creases spill over the fat white folds
Of your jaded brown limbs.
Under the layers of torn silk.
Touching your raised skin.
Shrouded. You keep your lids sewn shut.
The moment, unfurling, presses itself open.

🔊 bit.ly/saw20threadbare

What I could never say   *Raisa Kabir*

Walking alone. Through hurried corridors.
Pulling at my fingers, eyes focused on the floor.
Shuffle shuffle; shuffle shuffle.
I stop.

Here will do just fine, by this pane
Of glass. That my head and fists
Fall and bang against. Sobbing into the window
As patients walk past.
Legs give way, and I'm collapsing.
Not moving. Just heaving.
No dignity to keep.

After waiting I finally see her.
Dr Baildam. Her hard, moulded face
And pleasant, patronising smile.
I want to scream and curse at her.
But I stay still and blankly stare.

She looks at my blackened eyes,
Asks if I've been crying?
'No', I say. My head gently shakes
The air.

🔊 <u>bit.ly/saw21neversay</u>

Untitled (Excerpt)   *Raisa Kabir*

She presses ink onto my fingers,
Stiff and swollen, midst of a flare up.
Labouring to fully stretch my hand.
She says I should have stayed at home.
She says I shouldn't have been out in the cold,
At a demo. Not with my condition.

A die-in at Westfield shopping centre,
A demo against police brutality.
Black lives matter! Hands UP! Don't Shoot!

But it's them that arrested us,
Kettled us, held us for hours
Beside the dual carriageway.

ACAB. ACAB. ACAB. ACAB.
Black lives matter! Hands UP! Don't shoot!

Joints buckling in pain.
Could I sit somewhere less cold?
The officer shouted Just sit down on the ground.
Muscles seized up, I collapsed.
A swarm of cops. I froze.
Aware of the state's hands on my disabled body.

🔊 bit.ly/saw22untitled

Wasting   *Raisa Kabir*

I am motionless for a minute or two,
Emotionless for slightly longer.
These jarring bones of mine fall heavily
Limp under swathes of tight skin.
Moistening my lips with the curve
Of your tongue.
Feebly moving my padded, cumbersome self.
Lying low, undressing the sore fastenings.
Lifting my stiff body out of malleable clothes.
Peeling my soft knees from my rolling tights:
Hot pink, too warm to touch.
Opening my disjointed legs, safely entwined by yours.
The slip of a shoulder, tightening the bent
Of my enclosing spine.

🔊 bit.ly/saw23wasting

"Often when trying to discuss physical disability, as well as living with an invisible one, the dialogue of linking mental and physical health in the medical world is a frustrating one. Living with physical disability often causes depression, and living with depression and anxiety often make your symptoms worse; and so the cycles are set in motion.

After living with rheumatoid arthritis and depression for thirteen years, and examining how my body has absorbed trauma and manifested itself as fibromyalgia, I am interested in how marginalised identities, who often bear the brunt of many oppressions, end up dealing with chronic pain and poor mental health in their lives, and this direct link of remembered violence, trauma and disability politically placed on the body.

These are a set of poems that try to map out varying points in the differing ways which we perhaps deal with and resist oppression, and its blaring impact on managing mental health. A small collection of the struggles that stem from the many experiences that are embedded within a queer brown disabled femme body.

Disability politics run throughout the work and inform every sentence, from literally holding plural intersecting identities, queer and femme, disabled and brown – these identities inform each other, and shape each other together – none are ever separate.

Everything I write is always informed by the ways I have negotiated my experience of survival. Be that the medical system, living with depression, internalised racism, being the child of immigrants, and plain old learning to live with chronic pain."

– Raisa Kabir

Rules

Pieces

Isha

It is that time again.
Whispers flutter and hush
the whoosh of her wheels,
the stomp of his sticks,
his droopy head too heavy
for his neck. 'But you know,
he could do a wee little job,
couldn't he, a few hours a week,
hmm? He can pick things up
and put them down, hmm?'

'Did he? *Did* she? Really?
Beachy Head, you say?'

Pretty lies paper the land,
slip into the sea, so delicately.
She takes them with her
and they are found, floating.

🔊 bit.ly/saw24pieces

Accommodation   *Cath Nichols*

They would like to be executives
in smart suits and ties but their faces
don't quite fit the corporate divine,

with their cleft noses, hooks for hands,
fur where others' skin is smooth. The room
booked for interview failed to provide

adaptations. Roosts. Bat applicants tried
to stand but dizziness ensued, then bumps
and bruises. I wish the senior manager

had seen those bats last night: wheeling, fast
and light across the evening sky, catching moths,
gnats on the tightest of curves, returning to roost

in the smallest of spaces, adept and economical.
Bats are beautiful and smart but will never
make the grade if we stick to polyester fibres,

keep up regulation offices, where
workers always stare askance
at fur and leather wings.

🔊 bit.ly/saw25accommodation

Wash your hands
before you leave toilet

Cath Nichols

*I have seen some individuals leaving the toilet without washing thier
hands, these people are rather extremely arogant and dirty as they
leave their genital germs on everything that they touch, those germs
are ingested/swallowed by others as they use or touch the same things
that these dirty people have touched without washing their hands.*

Circled in thin, red pen: 'thier' and 'arogant'.
Red observes a 'run on sentence' and judges
'6/10 see me.' A further comment in thick black ink:
'Nice to see OCD is still prevalent amongst the academic classes.'

We live too close and side by side.

thier   arogant

 bit.ly/saw26wash

Migration of the Brown-Grey Unicorn   *Cath Nichols*
Leptonycteris yerbabuenae

Cumular volcanic ash, we rise
as shoals of fish, strength in numbers,

mesmerise our predators then
travel north to mate.

Each night we feed on nectar, pollinate
tequila flowers. Our bellies swell

heavy with babies. Further north
we dunk our upper bodies

into goblet flowers of cacti.
The birthing cave is almost underground

and in its farthest caverns we hang
hairless jelly babies upside-down,

pink sugar mice that oscillate.
Each newborn pup's umbilical

strikes a brown vertical,
shivering withered grasses

that vibrate with tender noise.

🔊)) bit.ly/saw27migration

Can You Help Me Let Me (excerpt) *Alec Finlay*

i/

what is this
   that has
      come into

the little
   space
      that I fill?

A MORE UN-
RECOGNISABLE SELF

illness

Words, poems: witness – ways to convince someone, and ourselves, that pain is comprehensible.

The effect of pain: pulled threads, frayed threads, threads that draw us apart – apart from time, apart from friends, apart from the world we have known and hope to know again.

We say we *bear* : it has a weight, and the spirit bears the imprint.

the it *within*
can become
a voice inside

Wellbeing is defined by the extent to which we can dwell with *'it'* within, or create an identity for ourselves without this *'it'*.

Our choices in the matter are often limited, given that *'it'* dwells within us and reaches without us.

One measure of wellbeing is the ability to translate *'it'* into speech or writing.

ii/

half-way
  to speaking

  takes us
part ways

out of
  loneliness

a borrowed walking
stick to make the sign
for what was
  happening

  still, no one saw

up there
where my legs
  can't go

the little that needs said
  when you meet

another person
  who shares
    the same condition

iii/

Fantasy: the revolution in medicine began at Stanford: a gentle professor of urology had a nurse inject him with a preparation that simulated the pain experienced by his patients. Things would never be the same again.

HAVING
THE SAME
CHAIR

equality

Robertson Davies gave this as one of his principles as a doctor: no desk closing him off from the patient, and no chair that is superior to theirs.

if there is pain
 in the room

then that pain
 is inside someone

if we did
not change
we would not
need one an-
 other

Calculation: if I rest *this* long will I be able to manage *that*?

Illness is an inequality – much more than an injustice.

iv/

Brecht blamed his heart condition on having been forced to listen to Chopin as a teenager.

He held the view that it was society's maladjustment and pressures, and the aggressive reduction of everything to modes of exploitation that was responsible for much ill health. He continued to believe, sincerely, that social revolution would bring about his own cure.

the test is
  a perfect terror

of now, soon,
  or never

a man walks in
to the social security system
and says
'I've come to be cured...'

The ill get campaigns, badges urging them to fight their condition and, paradoxically, they are never more praised than when they are running marathons. But, when the time comes, they receive no Remembrance Day, and no medals.

A friend tells me of one assessment centre which is known to regulars as 'Lourdes'.

The memory has never left me: standing before a glass partition, trying to explain to an official of the DSS – as they were known then – that my illness meant that I could work for around 15 hours in a week, but I could not predict *which* 15 hours.

limits are reached
at different speeds

Silica   *Georgi Gill*

contains found text from Frans Vermeulen's
Prisma: The Arcana of Materia Medica Illuminated

Looking back, no one recognised the early signs;
your dreams of swallowing needles, waking each day
with pricking tonsils till you started sleeping with a pebble
of quartz stowed under your tongue. It sucked you up,
taught you to expect less, try harder, but the rules shifted
and were not fair.

Now you find sand daily, a grainy itch in your socks,
in the crease of a bra seam, the gusset of your knickers –
evidence of a beach trip that will not happen this summer.
You are cast in sand. When the doctors lift the bucket,
you start to crumble; soft, silicate, out of shape.
It progresses and you learn that progress is not
always positive. You shed thin, granular trails
if you walk too far, too hard, too fast. The rules shift
and are not fair so, in case of leaks, you keep
a dustpan in your bag.

You are your own flint rations so you learn to measure,
eke out your grains. You'll always expect less, sometimes
try harder. They, it, you keep failing but you'll learn
to be thrifty, to step round puddles of sympathy
but when you slip, you'll mop it up, isolate it in your lungs,
you'll hold your breath. You'll stop your ears with cotton wool
to stop your thoughts drifting; you'll try to stitch
your word-grains together. But everything must slip.
Expect less, try harder. They, it, you must fail
so fail well, fall well, try to fall with care
if you know you fall at all. The rules
will shift; they will not be fair.

🔊 bit.ly/saw28silica

Georgi Gill
A drawn out magic trick

It's a drawn out magic trick: now you see her;
now you... still see her, only slightly less,
a little blurred around the edges,
quieter too, she forgets more
than you ever saw, rubbed
out bit by bit; now
you see her;
now you

🔊 bit.ly/saw29magic

"I have relapse remitting MS, and find there is a constant tension between society's expectations to either 'overcome the odds and beat the enemy of disease' or accept 'failure' and be ill quietly.

My dis/ease is part of me, physically and mentally, and, while not all of my poetry deals explicitly with this subject, it clearly informs the themes and process of my writing – I don't think I could write truly in my own voice if it didn't."

– Georgi Gill

The Chalice and the Heart   *Rose Cook*

He explained as clearly as he could
about the heart inside each vertebra.
He drew, and it was beautiful,
the spinal cord rising through a series of hearts.

One of mine is no longer a heart
but a chalice, like a cocktail glass.
Eventually, it may shrink to the rune
Algiz, the earth, which is also Z the end.

In Recovery   *Rose Cook*

I spend most of the days in a kind of recovery position.
The floor is littered with objects. Once dropped, they must stay
there until someone can retrieve them – pills, pencils, apples,
soap.

During the night, I am sustained by the stations of the clock. I
flick on the radio to hear an American woman talking about the
Cassini space mission. Their craft has been studying Saturn,
circling space for years to collect data. Soon it will be time to end
its flight with a grand finale crash, landing on the planet's face.
Until now they've avoided the Rings, because their molecular
dust could damage the sensors. She says it will be exciting
to direct their craft through the Rings on a last sacrificial voyage.
She said 'sacrificial'. She said 'exciting'.

I lie curled, wonder about them sending junk to another planet. I
fall into sleep, pass through forgotten ghosts. We must protect the
under-dream of existence, catch life working through us, expect
angels in luminous freefall, turning through space.

dlrow   *Sarah Golightley*

d l r o w
transfixed I look over
;or

                              Does not look tired.

measure myself against
rise towards
oscillation of

                              Average build.

quality of life questionnaire
body / movements, moments

                                   Well kempt.

de-finite definitions
d l r o w
rendition efface
marked

                              Casually dressed.

dubbed not duped
not your subjugate

                         Normal facial expression.

knuckles cracking
tick box; ticking
shadows of you

                              **Interaction normal, not
                         restless or withdrawn.**

d l r o w
atos an autocorrect
musn't grumble
you fill the range

                         Coped well at interview.

trickle down effect
insipid able bodied
orchestra of temporary

                              Adequate rapport.

pawned, you
depart, meant
shell of social care

Adequate eye contact.

d l r o w
i cannot dream to
see how you would
wind, role reverse

Normal amount of speech.

sourced your lacking
cut throat austerity
brain fog is a mind-pillow

Speech content was normal.

tally ratios, casual causal
interference of inference
don't just take my word
for it / we can eat science

**Behaved normally, not
hostile, or withdrawn.**

concretise individuals
coded by numbers
d l r o w
you will know how de-
i am

Orientated in time, place and person.

position to, hypermobile
swelling up to resistance
medication, sweet corn

Did not require prompting.

the cogs of you and i
in room protected
by barbed wire
and daily mail's

Adequate general memory.

d l r o w
disjointed assimilation
belly, rumbling, in my
butterfly museum stomach

        Adequate concentration.

the universal human
hand outs, not change
we are w/e, hashtag
no hand out either

        Able to remember three objects after
        a few minutes (normal).

i cannot rain nor cloud
but sleep like adversity
see riots through the window

        Able to spell 'world' backwards.

d l r o w
reblink existence
counting my spoons
aggregates

        Able to calculate correct change when
        asked sum.

germinating
dissent co-opted, flourish
like paralympians'
rights, denied, with smiles
applause

        Able to complete five rounds of several sevens.

in theory
fuck this
drink tea

        Has good insight into her illness.

 bit.ly/saw30dlrow

Name
Deserving Disabled Chronic Illness Resume
Postal Address | Telephone Number | E-mail Address

Profile
Open with your illness summary; two lines, catchy, to the point. Follow on with three bullet points, outlining most significant qualifications that establish your credentials. For example:

- Formal diagnoses, medication and 'treatments'.
- Your genuine inability to have health conditions fixed by just going for a walk.
- Proportion of human to disabled that you are, can be fluctuating.

Pain Matrix
As a Deserving Disabled, you will undoubtedly have a lot of information gathered on symptoms, discrimination and daily tasks you are unable to do without causing yourself pain, which will often span in excess of many years. To be able to streamline this experience and bring to the forefront the pain, anger and fatigue you have, it is always beneficial to include a Pain Matrix, which details straightaway the areas in which you have been fucked over. Such as:

Muscle weakness | Fatigue | Anxiety | Diarrhoea/Constipation | Fainting | Injuries | Drowsiness | Memory loss | Weight gain/loss | Depression | Aches and pains | Hearing loss | Post-Traumatic stress | Blurred vision | Inability to walk/stand | Desire to gouge your eyes out | Muscle inflammations | Insomnia /Hypersomnia | Migraines | Hormonal imbalance | Psychosis | Dizziness | Tumours | Insatiable open and bleeding wounds | Ensemble of deficiencies | Cancers and so on...

Personal Attributes
Describe your character here (no more than three bullet points), avoid discussing if you are trans*, queer, a survivor of violence, that your family is from a perceived 'developing country', as they will see

this as the root cause of all your problems. Proclaim your desire to contribute to capitalism.

Career Detail

Condition 1 – **MEDICATION AND TREATMENT**   **Dates**
Start your career disabled experience with a short paragraph that demonstrates daily duties that you can't do without assistance, without pain/injury, or death.

- Break down your lack of daily accomplishments in bullet point form so they stand out.

Condition 2 - **MEDICATION AND TREATMENT**   **Dates**
Continue with condition history until complete. Concentrate on the last 10 years of conditions, pains and losses. List older conditions in such a way that resilience cannot be inferred.

Surgical Development - At Deserving Disabled level, the chances are that your body started getting fucked up a long time ago; it is therefore a good idea to include any long-term impacts that you have accumulated to demonstrate that your body is dedicated to preventing full recovery.

Evaluations - MRIs, X-rays, blood tests, stool samples, blood pressure tests, heart beats per minute, etc., as well as any other evaluations gained whilst sick, such as Psychiatric Assessments, Safegarding Alerts, and the bullshit referral letters where they misrepresented everything you said.

Hobbies and Interests - Include all the activities you are no longer able to partake in as they are not accessible enough to you. Individualise your lacking, do NOT critique society for inaccessibility.

References are available on request.
References may be in the form of cat videos.

We are not all in this together.

🔊   bit.ly/saw31cv

I Am Hive

Gram Joel Davies

The pest guy was awkward, said
they are not here. The doctor
recommended the pest guy.

The cream did nothing.

I shaved my body bald.
Burnt every outfit but this one.

We are like a family
secret, they and I.
Under the microscope
I must resemble pumice,
and do not bother to scratch now.

By their feelers I know them.
They flinch into follicles
when the light switch flicks.

Textbooks never mention
this ecology. No one is telling.
Most likely, I am their sole niche:
something specific in my grease.

Once, I closed a jar on one.
It vanished through the glass.

🔊 bit.ly/saw32iamhive

Creep   *Gram Joel Davies*

Your carpet crawls like droplets on a hotplate.
The fear of tiny mouthfuls grows exponential
to fleabites.

Your TV fizzes, and news is, scroungers
piggyback our sweet creatures: a country
flakes to skin.

You go outside, where dog walkers pointedly
claw at the dole office. Suspicion
crawls up you

as you back for home. Through the curtain,
every curtain on the street fidgets
like carpet fibres.

🔊 bit.ly/saw33creep

"Living with a mental illness, an unseen disability, in a climate of political judgement, and an overarching air of estrangement, has been an uncomfortable way to exist. With constant rhetoric about 'scroungers' in the media, my feelings of paranoia, guilt and being outcast grew.

The 'fleas' implicit in my poem, 'Creep', are parasites. I hope to create the sense that even home does not feel quite safe. Out in the world, there is immense social pressure to present an acceptable face – a need for concealment. It can feel as if all eyes are on you, looking for reason to blame, to reveal the pest.

I personally have had people stare at me hard while making harsh remarks about those on benefits, with the sense that my agreement with their opinion, or its lack, was being scrutinised. What is paranoia, when the judgement is often real?"

– Gram Joel Davies

Prep Work with Overture   *Khairani Barokka*

She weatherproofs the sculpture, biting
her tongue indented, because here the wood
is imposing, but also fretful,
        fragile.
Children have strong, taut fists.

This piece was inspired by a garden her father
had kept from rot,
        is meant to be
steeped outdoors. How to ensure no vandals
pale the flush of completion.

Desecration of her work
calls to mind the Trickster's relation
to myth as a whole, the role of unknowable
mischief in the universe, all the intent
of an artist
        ripped to shreds.

Make things hardy while a hurricane
creeps on the peninsula, unannounced.

Tearing things down,
        like the stolen laptop,
like the weight of an old man's hand on hers
without life.
Like waking with the roosters
and choosing to chisel while ancestors
blow the quick brisk of their years
down your neck,

        and you make a space
in the indentations of fallen trees
and the cavity behind your lips,
        for fear.

🔊) bit.ly/saw34prep

Artist Statement

Khairani Barokka

When I'd whittled the first miniature, he had left the night before. I'd felt violent, which is a human emotion, and this is how I'd channeled it, with the gouging of pockmarks on tiny kindling. Those elvish arcs at the tops of the ears, those were what his had looked like. I'd intended destruction, and, instead, created in his image.

Work in a stupor, then in a trance, then seemingly in dreams – my sleep disorder run riot, a dangerous secret to harbour from the intricate knifing of wood.

Everyone had tried to call the house, then had assumed me on another trip to the shore for supplies. When my brother knocked, I'd held my breath.

Fifteen figurines later: all of my loves in a row. I had lost my day job. It was time to ring a friend from school who'd begun to work at a gallery.

 bit.ly/saw35artist

Okka to Marina   *Khairani Barokka*

Woman to woman.

I couldn't get into the Serpentine,
but I stared at you
sitting at the MoMA in 2010,
from the sidelines, no tears.
Short hair, glasses?
You wouldn't remember.

You did it, Marina.
We felt your soul ground anchor.

This is an urgent note:
regarding the navel star
carved into your flesh,
that preceded giving a heart to Ulay
for nursing your wounds
(sweet-child, archetypal falling-for).

I could not see you at the Serpentine.
No. More accuracy required:
I did not attempt it.
The lines were too long, and I tend
to harbour post-traumatic humming
sessions, induced by a week of feeling
as though someone is stabbing me,
invisible, and people walk by as it happens
and ask me how I am,
as silent marauder makes his incisions.
This illness of pain induced by
tiredness, strange luck,

what feels like a knife. My scarred teacher.
The blade stays in for a long time, Marina.
We nurse our own wounds
when everyone else has gone.

We must ration how we use
our hours of active duty,
with certain nervous systems,
and honestly,
I'd rather draw my fingers
across the hairs of my arm,
along the grain,
learn to cook asinan
in a sitting position,
or rock a friend's child,
heavier and heavier,
than wait in line for you to touch me,
and teach me about mindfulness.

Though it sounds heavenly.
Though I could probably make myself
ruin the exhibit by reading you this poem
in the instant in which you brush my shoulders.

Many of us other women
in the attempt of Performing Art
feel the searing of pain
with inevitability like the weight of air.
Beg for it to leave, ego in shreds.

The coven stars on our bellies lack scars.

I wanted you to know,
when I think of 'Rhythm 0' and I cringe,
I think of how waiting in line
at the Serpentine would have cost a body
an aggravated assault,
of torture by an unseen assailant
operating through the nerves,
and I'd close my eyes
and imagine strangling it,
wake up in the morning
with its nails coagulating with my blood –
the cost of seeing you
with your legacy of stabbing violence
of the kind that people see and understand,
and how you'd never know.

Just wanted you to know.

Please say hello to Jay-Z.

🔊 bit.ly/saw36okka

Circus   *Cathy Bryant*

The lights go up on bad dreams of a stunt man, a stunned man
and silent people in black who might be ninjas or stagehands.
Roll up, roll up, do you have a light, mate? Smoke clears
to reveal the magician and his assistant breaking up,
sawing their relationship in half. The Ringmaster's dressed
for hunting, taking bets on the trapeze artist's survival,
and which animals will later be whipped and chained;
shades of the sex games the Strong Man plays with himself.
To make it more exciting there's no safety net. Jump, jump,
the audience shouts to the bemused contortionist.
How? Which way? How high? Exit left pursued by
a bareback rider, bare, a bear, and a smell of things trapped
like mice in sawdust and the Big Top a cat,
a big top hat. Rabbits are pulled out, some dead.
We remember, with nostalgia, bread.

To My Non-Disabled Lover   *Cathy Bryant*

Greater than the la-la love of flowers,
chocs and soppy, poppish songs
is the hard bone and muscle of you
when I need power.

The hand, fluent with anger, filling in
court forms to sue discriminatory bastards;
the silent, endless work, the regular meals
and none of it seen as sacrifice,
not even the cleaning and scrubbing for me,
your gutter potentate.

'It's for us', you say. 'It's what we do.
Everything is for us. That's that.'
Not exactly a sonnet, but better
– and I'm left, no burden, instead queen
to your passionate king, fierce as hell.

Ms Bryant is Dangerously Delusional *Cathy Bryant*

from statements said or written about me and/or my partner, Keir

They keep the curtains closed.
The plumber will say of the claimant's partner, 'He wouldn't let me go
    upstairs to check the radiators.'
Other people have found Keir T. to be brusque or even threatening.
We were escorted by Keir T. and a 'friend', who weighing between
    18-20 stone was clearly intended to be intimidatory.
They always keep the curtains closed.

Catherine Bryant was (or was feigning to be) asleep.
I believe she is falsely claiming benefits.
Therefore I was justifiably angry.
I have had to give the claimant a wide berth, as her inventive malice
    and the belligerence of her partner causes me to feel nauseated.
The claim is fabricated. The claimant is irrational, vindictive and
    dangerously delusional.
If she can write a letter then she's not that disabled.
In spite of all her disabilities she was able to visit Heptonstall Graveyard –
    to visit a grave.
You seldom see the curtains open.

These videos show her speaking readily and adjusting her clothing
    whilst holding a glass.
She was apparently well enough to judge a poetry competition.
She is pulling the wool over the taxpayers' eyes.
She has taken every opportunity to pursue me with an excess
    of vindictive communications.
She used falsehood in an attempt to justify all the fabrications
    and exaggerations with which she embellishes her accusations.
        After all, she does claim to be a 'creative writer'.
We do not dispute that Ms Bryant is disabled.

She has made an occupation of tailoring disability to her advantage.
I am probably not her first, nor her last victim.
She keeps the curtains closed.

🔊 bit.ly/saw37msbryant

"Disability informs my poetry because it is part of who I am and how I live my life and perceive the world, and also part of the way that the world sees me. For example, when articles on writing suggest 'going for a walk and observing nature', they assume that the reader can see and walk. I might be lying in bed, and the closest I can get to nature is staring at the orange on my lunch plate. Well, that's fine – there aren't many poems about staring at oranges, and does the world really need yet another poem about observing the transient beauty of spring flowers?"

– Cathy Bryant

Audience   *Sandra Alland*

The poem knows how to enter a room. It's wearing a sans serif
22-point font: a sexy Verdana that complements your Arial. The poem
displays its bright yellow on a sleek black background, offers you
blue acetate to drape over glaring white. 'Remember me', signs the
poem. 'I am your audience. Remember me, I am yours.'

The poem will speed up or slow down, give you a transcript, let you
leave and come back later – if you feel like it. It takes you by the hand
or elbow or chair-handles, nods or writes a secret word if you don't
like to be touched. In your lap Braille appears, and on your ears
a headset: sound loop installed, audio cued. The poem leans on
its crutches to study you, smiling.

You and the poem click. You glide as one down the portable ramp
the poem brought in its pocket. Together you install an electric exit
button, escape bad lighting and the choke of noise and perfume.
The doors burst apart, and there's only this moment. The poem
whispers (with captions): 'Forget them, fuck them.'

🔊   bit.ly/saw38audience

Unparalleled poetic assistance into the Canon UK[*]   *Sandra Alland*

Cheek to cheek achieve talking.
Talk talk talk talk talk ///
            talking 'household'. Bucking,
            looking.

As acts you act a cheap act
;
            every time I sneeze
            you fold up
;
            I didn't say talking and you know it.

Catch all witches, cheap each cheque   :   :   :
            [[[peace of chit for Buckingham]]]

I have hayfever. You, acyl.
Acyl, as told at school ///
            asks on hold,
            asked whole,
            passel as hole.

How the flock Mac but don't talk.

And she she she she adds ///
            but that I keep back,
            to ask you your fault.

[*] Not that kind of cannon. (That neither.)

🔊   bit.ly/saw39canon

96

The Unforgotten, or
Mary do you want to talk about last night

Sandra Alland

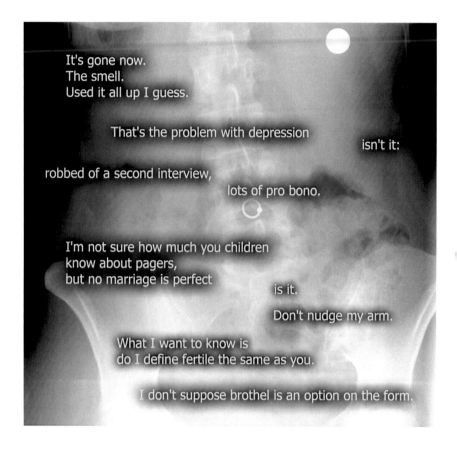

It's gone now.
The smell.
Used it all up I guess.

That's the problem with depression

isn't it:

robbed of a second interview,

lots of pro bono.

I'm not sure how much you children
know about pagers,
but no marriage is perfect

is it.

Don't nudge my arm.

What I want to know is
do I define fertile the same as you.

I don't suppose brothel is an option on the form.

  bit.ly/saw40unforgotten

p.227

 p.228

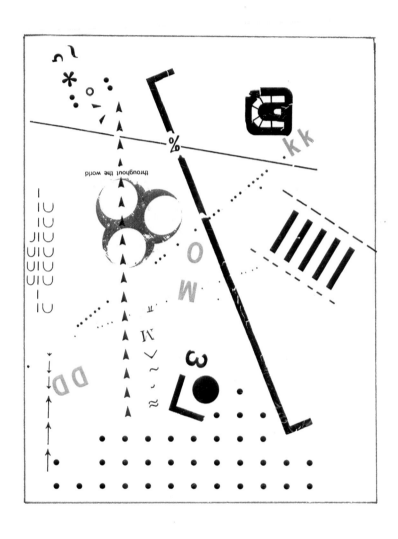

 p.228

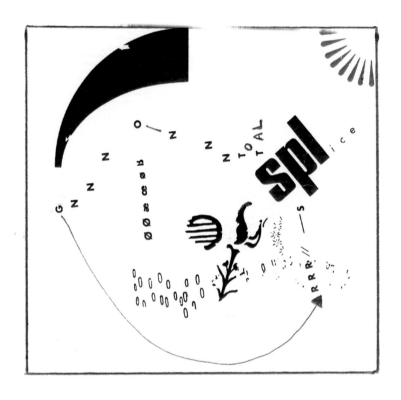

 p.228

Could It Just Be   *Aaron Williamson*

Dense sensations inside a farm animal

Announce themselves

At mutant scrapyards

Wraparound bilious

Each of it good

And full of emphysema

Rat crap, debris, icing cake

Old gone-off rope

Fine stuff

Whom calm invades

Edging into some

Boat-locked febrility

That's wearing tied boots slung

Round sixth-sense shoulders

Braced for sunsets

Over apples from the vine

Could it just be

Yet more likely

At the heart of the ash-heap

You'll simply rattle along your

Loose piano-frisking self

Now that it's not that what counts

Maps

A Language We Both Know   *Raymond Antrobus*

Most of my school life played out in Special Educational Needs units. From six years old it was assumed I was dyslexic and introverted. It wasn't until the phone rang while I was sitting in my mum's kitchen one day that she realised I was totally oblivious to the shrill, high-pitch sound. This changed the pathology on my school reports from 'slowness' to 'deafness'.

It's our first seven years of life that are vital for our language acquirement, most of which comes from what we pick up through hearing. Without my deafness diagnosed there were holes in my relationship with sound. When SEN teachers assessed me in class, I would strain to hear everything (even with hearing aids), feeling my intellect was being questioned; the pressure quickly hurt my brain. By the second lesson I'd be trying not to fall asleep. (Once it was noted my dad was Jamaican, it raised the question whether I was smoking weed.)

Despite the anxiety of school I kept a journal and wrote in notebooks, which is how I subconsciously preserved and built my love and confidence of language. What followed was years of speech therapy, audiology clinics and five years in Blanche Nevile Deaf School (with most lessons taking place in the hearing school next door with support teachers). In both hearing and Deaf spaces I was defensive about my ability to communicate. I began learning BSL, but the hearing students began teasing me when they saw me speaking it. On the other side of the wall some Deaf students mocked my lack of BSL fluency, calling me a 'baby signer.'

Regardless, I wanted to identify as hearing, so I began wearing hats over my hearing aids or sneaking them out of my ears in class. Looking back this was when I most needed the nurturing of a Deaf identity, one that wasn't medical, but philosophical, one that embraced my natural love of language and valued Deafness as a way of being.

So why have I turned to poetry to publicly explore this? Because poems are careful things, if done well, every sound and word has something to carry. My poems are Deaf poems because they are defiant in how they take up space on the page, not searching for loss, but for something gained. A poem like 'All I Hear Is Your Gaze' says listen to yourself, the way you speak to me, this is the kind of language I've had to read from your lips, but look, I hold it up and reflect it back to your eyes and ears – aren't you the one that is verbally strange / funny?

In 2015 I wrote a play called *A Language We Both Know*, which was put on at The Roundhouse. It was a series of autobiographical poems / spoken word monologues looking back at my time in Deaf / hearing education. I collaborated with CODA, Charmaine Wombwell as director, and Deaf actor / BSL interpreter, Rezene Woldeyesus. Being a poet in residence for six months at Blanche Nevile Deaf School and meeting students (some of whom were going through similar struggles I had growing up between the D/deaf and hearing worlds) prompted the writing of the show.

'Dear Hearing World' was written after my first day, meeting a year seven student who told me he had gotten into a fight because a hearing student made fun of his cochlear implants. The situation was dealt with by a number of compassionate teachers who went on to organise an assembly for the hearing school, led by D/deaf teachers who spoke about their experiences and taught the students some signs. This moved me, nothing like that happened to me at school. I remember being told to 'just ignore it' (by hearing teachers). This example confirmed that it can only be us, the D/deaf voices, that can act and be heard as we are – *we can't hear our joints crack but we can feel them*.

🔊 bit.ly/saw41language

106

No Body to Write With: Intrusion as a Manifesto for D/deaf and/or Disabled Poets

Abi Palmer

Introduction

The book has somehow to be adapted to the body... women's books must be shorter, more concentrated... so that they do not need long hours of steady and uninterrupted work.

— Virginia Woolf, A Room of One's Own

There have been so many valuable responses raised to Woolf's limited understanding about what it means to be a 'woman' (white, educated, cissexual), and yet significantly fewer regarding what it means to have a body. Whilst acknowledging the shortcomings arising even in the quote above, I still find myself drawn to this idea of a literary form that must somehow 'be adapted to the body'. What of disabled bodies? What type of writing belongs to us?

If, in 1928, the financially independent and well-educated Woolf argues that a woman who is to write must have 'money and a room of her own' in order to avoid the physical and mental interruptions of place, obligation, and decorum, how, almost a century later, is the disabled writer supposed to find their ground? The physical and/or mentally disabled person is so often severely limited by the boundaries of body and mind: the intrusion of pain, fatigue and brain fog; adverse reactions to medical trials; and flare ups or chronic lows that come and knock you out for days and months at a time. Intrusion is such a part of many disabled people's lived experience that no amount of space, time or financial freedom would ever be able to fully compensate.

But a shift has occurred. Where Woolf argues that her 20th century (white, cis, middle-class) female students need to overcome their contextual interruptions in order to join the grand literary canon, it is precisely the *refusal* of 21st century disabled poets to shy away from their everyday intrusions that makes the movement so outstanding. Intrusion is the literary driving force for radical transformations in how language and context are applied: in the rhythm, pace and imagery; in the poem's form, its shape, external and internal additional inputs.

As a 'writer' who intermittently loses the use of her hands (through pain, muscle weakness and autoimmune responses), I find myself increasingly unable to skirt around these intrusions, laboriously chipping away at this essay over a two-month period, on a touchscreen DVORAK keyboard they don't make anymore. At moments where the pain intensifies, I find myself revisiting a poem from *Stairs and Whispers*:

> I tried to love you, but you laughed at my deaf grammar, I used commas not full stops because everything I said kept running away, I mulled over long paragraphs because I didn't know what a 'natural break' sounded like, you erased what could have always been poetry (strike that out).

– 'Dear Hearing World', Raymond Antrobus

Although many D/deaf people consider the D/deaf body in a manner distinct from a disabled framework, I cannot help but see parallels in the intrusions the poem describes. Antrobus presents, better than any 'abled' or 'hearing' poet I have found, the undeniable pain faced by identifying as a writer when the literary canon has not been designed to accommodate your experience of 'writing'. His poem is built from intrusion: every strike, every 'uncorrected' comma a bursting out, a rejection of a form that has dismissed his own truth. 'You erased what could have always been poetry' is a blueprint for why it is so important for D/deaf and/or disabled writers to 'write back'. Accepting intrusion into the body of a poem becomes a catalyst for innovation, a series of unexpected ruptures. As I lie awake at night, waiting for my fingers and wrists to recover, I vow to myself that this essay will be the last time I allow a literary form to outweigh the experience of my own body.

I. Literary Intrusions

Intrusion comes in many forms through *Stairs and Whispers*. Take Nuala Watt's combination of sensory deprivation and overload in 'Receiving My Poems in Braille': 'Nobody else touched sound, / so I shuddered away from the raised dots / that captured my name'. The lines may be read simply: a frank acknowledgement of coming to terms with 'othering' blindness and its physical manifestation in the form of Braille. But, more than this, the poem reflects a sensory intrusion: of touch replacing sight. This is an intrusion on the narrator's ability to 'become lost' in the world of written word, a straddling of language and sightlessness. The visceral 'shudder' at 'raised dots' invites sighted and non-sighted readers alike to explore the potential of language as an experience of sensory overload. In providing a tangible example of what it means to 'touch sound', Watt provokes an alternate state of synaesthesia. The intrusion of touch and sound within a poem of blindness causes us to reconsider our understanding of the word 'noise'.

This is not the inspiration-porn, 'overcoming' of disability that clutters the mainstream narrative: disabled as Paralympian, disabled as hero, in spite of their 'disadvantages'. Nor is it the 'poetry as therapy'/'disabled as victim' rhetoric. ('Sure, it's great that they're writing, but is it actually good?') The poem excels in its textural richness, leading us to a conclusion that is neither positive nor negative, but simply *is:*

My thoughts have arrived in the post.
I guess I'm somewhere, embossed.

By the end of the poem, whilst the intrusion is anticipated, it is significant that the conclusion is moderated with ambivalence: 'I guess'.

This form of acknowledgement may be read as a frank, almost neutral feature of the disabled writer's practice. 'My disability is an inevitable, completely mundane fact that I see no reason to deny... It's how I live experience,' writes poet and activist Markie

Burnhope.[3] But the invitation to explore one's physical presence with such bluntness is a radical movement away from cultural attempts to escape, overlook or sweeten the narrative of the disabled body. Burnhope uses the simple example of acknowledging movement through space: 'I sometimes write "I wheeled" rather than "I walked"'. The transformation of this single verb produces a dramatic alteration in the pace, rhythm, and even height of the reader's literary perspective. By shifting beyond the culturally romanticised role of writer as walker, mover and flâneur, the disabled poet creates a new paradigm, simply by stating the truth of their lived experience.

Of course, the perspective of the disabled body often intersects with that of other intruded-upon identities. This has the potential to bring with it an increased wave of literary collisions, perhaps most apparent in the work of (self-described) 'South Asian Queer Crip Femme (of Colour)' Raisa Kabir. In 'Threadbare', the vocabulary of invasion takes up approximately 60% of the overall word count. Violent and tactile imagery: 'impales', 'stitches', 'Embedded', 'Torn', 'Shrouded' and 'Sewn' create a piling-on of physical ruptures, a multiplicity of intrusions, significant to a body likely to have been forced to justify its presence on multiple fronts. But while dense with pain, the poem is also overwhelmingly intimate. The 'fabric' of Kabir's language hangs in a delicate juxtaposition: 'failing seams' may simultaneously fall apart and burn from the stitches which attempt to bring them back together. Intrusion is woven into the very body of the poem, both necessary and uncomfortable.

And yet, when I read the stanza again, it occurs to me that perhaps its purpose could be completely the opposite: perhaps it wants to fall apart and is fighting not to. The poem ends in release: 'The moment, unfurling, presses itself open.' Is this aching, or ecstasy? It occurs to me too that for the writer in pain, the relationship between the two is often inescapable.

---

[3]   Brown, Phil, 'Wider Reading: Interview with Markie Burnhope', http://discoverilove.blogspot.co.uk, accessed August 17, 2011.

II: Technology and Intrusion

The stage is set for a growing acceptance of such intrusions on the rhythm, pace and style of current disability poetics through the rapid expansion of artificial intelligence software. Nowhere is cultural Innovation more interesting to humanity than when it can be used as a vessel to explore one's own 'true' self. And nowhere does artificial intelligence become more truthful than when it fails us. Little flaws and idiosyncrasies in the mind of a computer appear to show us something about our own minds. This is explored in 2010, by experimental poet Ross Sutherland, as he considers the poetic effect of flawed machinery in a 'collaboration' with digital translation software:

When you say to a translation program X=Y, the computer thinks 'OK, X is Y' and smashes the two things together. This is always the moment of catalyst, when the translator steps in and takes over the text. From the chaotic crossbreeding of metaphors, a new narrative logic emerges, and the poem moves off in a new direction.[4]

In other words, it is the intrusion, the inability for the computer to act and think like a 'normal' person, that excites the literary reader, and creates the surprise and innovation in these collaborations. Like the irregular shape of a leaf in the natural world, or the sharp cliff contrast against an ocean horizon, it is the flaw, the juxtaposition, and surprise of line that allows for a moment of originality in 21st century poetics.

To revel in rather than conceal these multiple mistakes and intrusions creates a broader space for the disabled and/or D/deaf writer to fill: the flawed, imperfect, rarely represented creature full of breaks and false starts. And the relationship between intrusion and technology is all the more important for the disabled poet, for whom this technology exists not only as a thought experiment, but as a means to an end.

---

[4]   Sutherland, Ross, 'Every Rendition on a Broken Machine,' *Stress Fractures: Essays on Poetry,* Chivers, Tom (ed.), Penned in the Margins, 2010 (with thanks to Tom Chivers for a late-night book loan at short notice).

Sandra Alland's 2012 text, *Naturally Speaking,* is a meditation on a relationship with voice recognition software. Like Sutherland, Alland regards the fractures in the software as a poetic 'collaboration', referring to the technology as a 'virtual me'. Likewise, it is again the flaws, the 'mashing together' of words and sounds that creates linguistic innovation, the delicate line between robotic surrealism and unexpected moments of human connection, that are most remarkable. In *Stairs and Whispers*, Alland continues to explore this relationship:

> Talk talk talk talk talk ///
> > talking 'household'. Bucking,
> > looking
>
> – 'Unparalleled poetic assistance into the Canon UK',
> Sandra Alland

Initially, these lines may appear absurd and nonsensical (if not full of rhythm). But later in the poem, we are presented with the line: 'I didn't say talk and you know it'. An unexpectedly 'human' breakthrough, the phrase causes another examination of the words that precede it. To a robot, could talking, bucking and looking not all sit as reasonable replacements for the incomputable 'fucking'? When this connection is made by the reader (whose brain, after all, has been granted permission to swear), is it not possible to begin to form other connections? When we know of the intention finely veiled beneath the repetition of 'talk talk talk talk', doesn't this manifest itself as a perfect act of foreplay? And isn't a fuck just another rhythmic act of communication? Connected by a computer's mistranslation, the talking, the bucking and the looking all become filthy and romantic, interconnected and important. When the association is made, one can almost feel the new neural pathways opening: a relationship forming between 'household' and fuck, both smutty and banal, obscene and everyday.

But whilst this creation of new metaphor ('household' = 'sex') may offer one's neurons a small moment of revolution, it is equally important to remember the rupture from which these connections were made. It is not difficult to imagine the writer, head to mouthpiece, swearing with increasing frustration, censored by the machine that is meant to provide assistance. Like Kabir's 'failing seams', again, the poem exposes the delicate line a disabled writer straddles between being held together and not wanting to fall apart.

III: Physical Intrusions

The 'room' that technology carves out, particularly for disabled writers, is an exciting one: collaborative, unafraid of ruptures, and embracing of fault. Social networking allows for a bringing together of a number of housebound and/or socially limited authors – a space to unite and see ourselves represented like never before. But I do not believe that this alone can provide the 'room' we require to flourish. Where 'death of the author' allows a role for machine as collaborator, *rise of the automatons* requires constant vigilance. Like so many parts of society, the cyber world is designed by the abled: a series of white, wealthy, Silicon Valley dudes with higher education and health insurance. The virtual world is so very biased, swamping us in the form of upclicks, weighing us down with its ad content and likes. There are limits in the power of technology to aid the disabled writer with their quest to carve out a space of their own.

In returning to Woolf's statement at the beginning of this essay 'the book must be adapted to the body', I am encouraged to think again of the role poetry has for a writer facing so many intrusions. A poem is the perfect medium for a disabled writer because it can be short, staccato and interrupted, or long and unpunctuated, unwieldy and out of control. Within its body, it can perform remarkable feats of language, perfect harmonies or entirely unexpected rules. But what is particularly exciting now, and for the future of disabled poetics, is the acknowledgement and acceptance of external physical context: the outside impact of intrusions on the way we read, write and perform poetry. Where postmodernism did its best to abandon context, the intruded-upon body refuses to be fully free. We – who may never fully escape into the world of a good book as we struggle to shift an uncomfortable elbow and prop ourselves painfully against pillows, dismiss the neurological tic or the uncomfortable humming in our left ear – instead of disembodying ourselves from this context, we have the opportunity to use it to push our work further.

In her lecture, 'My Body Is a Prison of Pain so I Want to Leave It Like a Mystic But I Also Love It & Want it to Matter Politically',[5] multidisciplinary writer Johanna Hedva invites listeners who do not face physiological intrusions to place a rock in their shoe as she speaks, to represent the perpetual background chatter of the body in constant argument with itself. We can analyse Hedva's action as an elaborate simile: 'chronic illness in the body is like a constant rock in your shoe'. But to experience it in a physical state allows the relationship to function more fully as an extended metaphor, physically present within every word. It transforms the listening experience, adding layers of distraction to a carefully-worded speech. Where experiments with 'interdisciplinary' media are rife throughout both arts and academia at present (to varying degrees of success), for the disabled writer, they present a particularly salient opportunity to expand upon and explore the significance of intrusion.

It is apt, then, to discover similar elements of this interaction in *Stairs and Whispers.* Consider the work of artist/choreographer Claire Cunningham: 'Her physical vocabulary comes from the study and use/misuse of her crutches'. The poems are extracts from live performances, creating a fascinating loop where the phrase 'i am on file. / you have the right to read me' was originally presented within the context of actual movement (where the body could truly be 'read'), but for the anthology, the text is repurposed into pure 'written' form, including a contextual note that allows the reader to imagine the poem as part of a physical dance involving crutches, and a link that allows them to listen to it as a song. Here, the language, movement and music are interconnected, referencing and reinforcing one another, yet each may perform independently, to produce an

---

[5]   Video version: Hedva, Johanna, 'My Body Is a Prison of Pain so I Want to Leave It Like a Mystic But I Also Love It & Want it to Matter Politically', *WCCW,* 2016. https://vimeo.com/144782433. An essay version of the lecture is also available: Hedva, Johanna, "Sick Woman Theory", *Mask Magazine,* 2015. http://www.maskmagazine.com/not-again/struggle/sick-woman-theory

entirely different effect. The triple use of the same piece of text is oddly liberating: for anybody who may struggle with the act of movement, listening or writing, producing one text with multiple outcomes feels like a multiple victory.

Similarly exhilarating is the visual interaction in Aaron Williamson's vispo (visual poetry) series, 'Tin Eaters': each 'poem' was made by concentrating for one hour on the tinnitus that he has 'learned to ignore'. Simply by refusing to engage with the societal rejection of his own daily lived experience, Williamson creates a landscape that can neither be read aloud in mere words, nor looked upon as a mere picture. A sense of movement is created: a buzzing, vibrating, physical intrusion of sound and non-sound on an otherwise white space. But it does not move at all. For an intrusion that presents itself in a distortion of how language is heard, it is necessary that the poem refuses to present itself in language alone.

And yet, for the visually-impaired or blind reader, this genre could provide further complication. In a recent interview with Claire Trévien, Giles L. Turnbull expressed his frustration at a suggestion that 'all poetry is visual poetry': 'If a poem was laid out in the shape of a teapot, a screen reader is simply going to read it as if it were a sentence in a page of Oliver Twist.'[6] The sheer volume and variety of D/deaf and disabled writers' lived experiences can create barriers to multidisciplinary or avant-garde work: how does one express the wordlessness of Williamson's aural experience to an unseeing gaze? In the case of *Stairs and Whispers*, this potential disconnect has been addressed with a written visual description of Williamson's pieces (available at the back of the book).

Whilst exact like-to-like depiction may not always be possible, consideration of each other's varying intruded-upon states invites a widening of linguistic (and super-linguistic) methodologies. For some, a verbal description of a rock in a shoe is less effective than simply putting one there; but opening the vocabulary of the disabled writer's toolbox to incorporate further multidisciplinary offerings can allow for

---

[6]   Turnbull, Giles L. and Trévien, Claire, 't-h-i-s-space-i-s-space-space-space-space-space-space', *Sabotage Reviews*, February 26, 2017, accessed April 14, 2017.http://sabotagereviews.com/2017/02/26/t-h-i-s-space-i-s-space-space-space-space-space-space-in-conversation-with-giles-turnbull/

a multiplicity of poetic exploration. After reading Turnbull's interview, I was encouraged to experiment with a recording of my poem, 'Doublespeak', which attempts to capture rather than describe the sense of overlap and conflict between found texts on a page that became caught in my printer. This is presented as part of an online collection of recordings from the anthology, and readers may also access a written and recorded descriptive text.

Likewise, Georgi Gill's recorded version of 'Silica' moves beyond verse form into an immersive soundscape: the aural droplets and echoes extending the seaside metaphor of the 'round puddles', the sucked pebbles and grains of sand within the text. When I listen, I find myself transported to a dark, wet, seaside cave from my own childhood. There is a sense of nostalgia, of darkness and loss, in this journey. In Gill's aural presentation of the poem, I find myself faced with a deeper understanding of how, in facing the experience of my own disability, 'the rules shifted / and were not fair.'

By foregrounding the impact of the intrusions experienced by its own writers, *Stairs and Whispers* is an anthology that expands the definition of what poetry is, what a book is, what a *body* is. Gary Austin Quinn's multilinguistic video, 'The stars are the map', is revolutionary in its sheer act of literally placing British Sign Language in the middle of its performance, forcing the Shetlandic and English written words to move around the poet, overlapping and intertwining with the waves he embodies. Simply challenging the position of BSL as an afterthought, an intrusion, placed at the side of (and covering parts of) the screen, creates potential for an entirely new dance between languages. What is equally exciting is that this poem again exists in multiple forms: the Shetlandic and English verbal recordings provide an entirely different poetic landscape to the silent, but linguistically multiplied, video format.

Again and again, we are greeted with examples of how much farther 'the book' can be adapted to the body. How, by taking these adaptations, these intrusions, as a jumping-off point rather than a necessary obstacle to 'overcome', we find ourselves faced with the potential of poetry to move beyond the locked room, the unapproachable staircase.

My hope for the present and future of disabled and D/deaf poetics is that these contextual intrusions will continue to manifest themselves, both in the body of the poem and outside of it. As you read and reread (or listen to, or watch) *Stairs and Whispers*, picture the writer with the rock in their shoe, or try placing yourself in different environments: a loud cafe or in a dark, cold room. Consider how the temperature of the space around us changes, how we understand the language of Raisa Kabir's 'My head gently shakes / The air'. Hearing readers, or those with memory of hearing, I invite you to listen for the aural accompaniment to Khairani Barokka's 'Prep Work with Overture'. How does it sound when accompanied by a violin? Or the sound of drum'n'bass? Of numbing silence? In a poem where the very title invites an aural accompaniment, what does it mean that the sound of one fails to materialise? How does this transform our understanding of 'Mischief in the universe, all the intent / of an artist / ripped to shreds'?

Disability poetics is a breeding ground of innovation and variety: of ruptures and chasms; poetry that performs, and is informed, by the infinite physical and neurological realities of the disabled body. Physical intrusion as an extension of metaphor serves only to extend these performances. We may own it because it has never *not* been present – like so many aspects of our lived physical and neurological experiences, we have simply been encouraged to dismiss it for too long. And no matter how many private spaces are bought or gifted to us to write in, or how many tools or extensions we are granted, we will never be free of the intrusion of our own disabled and/or D/deaf reality in an abled, hearing world. This is a truth that we must continue to reclaim.

> 'Remember me', signs the poem. 'I am your audience,
> Remember me, I am yours.'
>
> – 'Audience', Sandra Alland

🔊 bit.ly/saw42nobody

Long Lost Lover

Bea Webster
Still: Ania Urbanowska

(silent, BSL with captions)
youtu.be/gmgbLvm-neQ

(BSL with voice-over, captions)
youtu.be/n5CNY3DWxws

English recording by Bea Webster:
  bit.ly/saw45longlost

  p.228

Turtlemen: Bishop in Love   *Andra Simons*
                                         Still: João Trindade

(audio with captions)
youtu.be/eoxrdaKIoK8

 p.229

The Stars are the Map

BSL: Gary Austin Quinn
Still: Kyra Pollitt
Translations: Christine de Luca and Kyra Pollitt

(silent, BSL with captions)

youtu.be/wFWbnjylyAY

Shetlandic recording by Christine de Luca:

🔊 bit.ly/saw44s-thestars

English recording by Christine de Luca:

🔊 bit.ly/saw43e-thestars

 p.229

Bilingual Poet's Dilemma

Donna Williams
Still: Ania Urbanowska

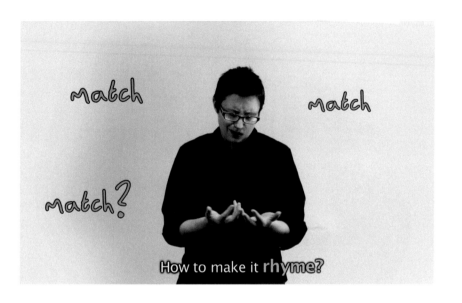

(silent, BSL with captions)

youtu.be/jackK3GmPHo

(BSL with voice-over, captions)

youtu.be/IJ-_L4f7LU8

 p.229

Am I Mentally Ill or Am I Just a Dickhead?

Jackie Hagan
Still: Mattr Media

(audio with captions)
youtu.be/Dufr9yrcrco

 p.229

Goat Poem (for the kids)   *Mark Mace Smith*
Still: Mark Mace Smith and Anigman

(audio with captions):
youtu.be/smdMsjMv1M4

 p.230

"In January 2015 I was living on a farm in Majorca, labouring for bed and food, and looking after a goat. I was not feeling much like a poet never mind a black one, but when asked to join the 'Black Poets Speak Out' movement I asked myself: 'If a black poet must speak out, what must a black poet speak out about and to whom?'

I believe that the main issue that can unite all peoples to get rid of this corrupt political elite is the public knowledge that members of parliament have been abusing children and have covered it up for decades.

'Goat Poem (for the kids)' is written to slice through the (news) fog and fear – the smoke and mirrors of terrorism that are created by those in power to divide us and distract us from our collective power. The poem evokes Charlie Hebdo, false flags, and the demonisation of Muslims – state-sponsored (UK/US) disinformation and fake news memes that hide the truth of our global political system.

The video came together from photographs and video that I took on a misty, Majorcan morning. The poem was written and recorded at the family home of the game designer and filmmaker, Anigman, who 'remixed' the video and images into this video/poem. The reference to 'honey on toast, strawberry jam on toast' is an observation of what his innocent children were eating when I wrote the poem. This is for The Kids."

– Mark Mace Smith

The Sword Swallower

Markie Burnhope
Still: Ania Urbanowska

(audio with captions)
youtu.be/R52vleBsQP8

 p.230

(audio with captions)
youtu.be/XJeuiaz9Gp8

 p.230

Kettle's Boiling

Alison Smith
Still: Sandra Alland

Can't you lipread?

(silent, some BSL with captions)

youtu.be/Vq1bKui9b9Y

 p.231

How can we identify a UK disability poetics?

Eleanor Ward

A community of 'crips'

I first discovered the community, and critical consciousness, that is disability poetics through Jim Ferris' ground-breaking essay, 'Crip poetry, or how I learned to love the limp'. I appreciated the idea of a community of poets who embrace the 'different place' that poetry by disabled people comes from, as well as rejecting the 'shameful, pitiable and tragic' perspective that disabled poets can experience.[7]

Ferris' essay argues that identifying as a disabled poet is invigorating. I wanted to be part of this group, almost as a form of protection. Disability poetics also acknowledges the importance of the social model of disability, which argues that 'disability is caused by the way society is organised, rather than by a person's impairment or difference'[8]; but, as Dan Goodley argues, disability poetics 'theorises beyond the social model'[9]. Like other critics, I had often found the social model took little account of issues affecting women or the chronically ill; through this expansion of its meaning I found a 'home' within disability poetics. I appreciated how disability poetics moved away from the 'inspirational' stories that populate many anthologies of poetry about disability and illness, and embraced poetry about and by disabled people, illustrating our individual experiences.[10]

---

[7]   Ferris, Jim, 'Crip Poetry, or How I Learned to Love the Limp', *Wordgathering, 1*, 2007.

[8]   Scope, 'The Social Model of Disability, What Is It and Why Is It Important?', 2016.

[9]   Goodley, Dan, 'Dis/Entangling Critical Disability Studies', *Disability & Society*, 28, 2013 (631-44).

[10]   Baird, Joseph L. and Workman, Deborah S., *Toward Solomon's Mountain: The Experience of Disability in Poetry*, Temple University Press; Mukand, Jon, *Articulations: The Body and Illness in Poetry*, University of Iowa Press, 1994; Denny, John Andrew, *Through Corridors of Light: Poems of Consolation in Time of Illness,* Lion, 2011.

UK approaches to disabled poets

My identity as a poet has been shaped by my disability, and also by my gender and its intersections with ethnicity/race and class. I have often considered the impact of my upbringing on my poetry. My experiences of growing up as a white English woman with Irish grandparents, as well as my educational background with its attendant privileges, have influenced how I write, and how my work is received.

I think I had a certain discomfort about embracing the role of 'disabled poet' at the beginning, preferring to distance myself from disability poetics because I was unsure what belonging to this group meant. Like many disabled people, I find the identity of 'disabled' fraught with complexity and difficult to define.[11] Similarly, D/deaf poets who do not identify as disabled also consider identity and language in their work with complexity. One of the consequences of this acknowledgement or rejection of identity is the possibility that it might change other people's perspective on your writing. Despite this, over the last few years, having learnt about disability poetics, I became invested in this type of poetry, and what this approach can do to further my writing. It makes me consider the politics of my writing, and asks me to reflect on how important art is in a world where austerity and disability hate crimes are becoming more common. Disability poetics allows writers to go beyond the social model, and gives permission to play with the idea of socially- and culturally-constructed conditions, and how we can safely challenge this idea. I enjoy knowing that my poetry is not only part of the disability rights movement, but also equally reflects how I personally see my identity and illness.

In the UK, despite gains in disability rights, including the Disability Discrimination Act in 1995, there has been little focus on the cultural influence of disabled poets. This is perhaps in part because of the reluctance of some UK poets to be defined in terms of their minority position, but also because of the lack of a unifying critical perspective on their poetry, which currently seems more common in US criticism of disability culture.

---

[11]   As deftly illustrated in: Shakespeare, Tom, *Disability Rights and Wrongs Revisited,* Routledge, 2013.

My interest in disability poetics has grown from devouring critics such as Petra Kuppers, who lived in Germany and the UK before moving to the US, and US-based Jim Ferris; these critics produce criticism and poetry that forces me to question where my perspective on a UK-led disability poetics lies. For some critics, such as Tom Shakespeare, the idea of a cultural disability studies, or disability poetics, is negatively received, and there is a move to disregard its importance. The collaborative nature of this anthology, and the included criticism, opposes the idea that only 'empirical social research' is important, and expands on the criticism that shows cultural representations of disability are equally powerful.[12]

Acknowledging a different history

I hope in many ways this anthology will renew local approaches to disability poetics. Up until now, there has often been a reliance on cultural representations of illness and disability in medical humanities or disability studies within the UK. Although this work highlights how important the stories of disabled people are,[13] poetry is markedly absent in discussions of how we can illuminate the political and sociological stories of disability. Disability poetics is also influenced by feminisms and the ways that women write about the body, and the subject of gender as a place for poetry and criticism has flourished in the UK. This perspective allows poets to challenge the identities of gender and disability simultaneously, and ask what defining an 'identity' means to them. This is important to my own work, where I digest the meanings of 'disabled' and 'woman', illustrating the complexities of both subjects.

As many critics, such as Margrit Shildrick, have noted, the combination of these two identities is fertile land from which to produce stories, as the two positions often feed into each other.[14] In

---

12   Ibid. (52).

13   Barnes, Colin and Mercer, Geof, *Exploring the Divide: Illness and Disability,* Disability Press, 1996.

14   Shildrick, Margrit, *Dangerous Discourses of Disability, Subjectivity and Sexuality,* Palgrave Macmillan, 2009; Shildrick, Margrit, *Leaky Bodies and Boundaries: Feminism, Postmodernism and (Bio) Ethics,* Psychology Press, 1997.

my own work, the ideas of relationships, gender and disability have allowed me to explore different perspectives (including that of society) on my own body, and to consider other women and non-binary people who may experience intersecting but distinct forms of prejudice including racism, cis/heterosexism, misogynoir and/or transmisogyny.

Medical Disability Poetry?

For many disabled poets, the social model of disability has an impact on their writing, and this perspective moves away from some of the discussion of medical narratives of illness or disability, wherein critics such as Thomas Couser interpret these narratives as 'healing.'[15] I strive to observe and communicate the difficulties of disability, instead of concerning myself with curative promises that go against the foundation of the social model of disability and disregard society's impact on our impairments.

The heart of a UK disability poetics will be found in the tensions between the social model, medical cure, and international political and cultural ideas about disability. Within the populations of four countries on many islands, poets of varied cultural, including non-white, backgrounds often author resistance to the homogeneity of a national poetics. UK-based poets are grappling with a social and cultural history that is in many ways 'new.' And although we all sit in the shadow of major historical events, such as the reemergence of the eugenics movement popular in the first part of the 20th century[16], for UK poets the recent history of disability, and the intersections between identity and poetry, lead to writing that is beautifully complex. In my own collections of poetry I am continually tackling how I understand disability. I use my poems to ask myself how medicine and the public experience of disability is so vastly different from how disabled people themselves experience it. My poetry also allows me to be upfront about my disability, which confronts how society can react with feelings of pity or shame. I use my poems to help disregard

---

[15]   Couser, G. Thomas, *Recovering Bodies: Illness, Disability, and Life Writing*, University of Wisconsin Press, 1997.

[16]   As foregrounded in Snyder, Sharon L. and Mitchell, David T, *Cultural Locations of Disability*, University of Chicago Press, 2010.

these cultural and emotional ways of seeing disabilities, and utilise disability poetics as a shield to protect me from the 'stares' that follow me around in my everyday life.[17] My poems allow me to bare all.

Finding a place to call home

My position as a disabled poet requires struggling with these conflicts between my identity and my writing. UK approaches to disability poetics are gradually developing, encompassing the juxtapositions of being uncomfortable with the label of disabled or 'crip', but also finding these labels liberating. I find the most invigorating part of my own poetry is treading the line between poetry that illustrates my position as a disabled woman, and how uncomfortable this same position can make me feel. I acknowledge the politics of writing in a misogynist world, and I know the social model is written into my poetry continually, as well as my individual criticisms of it, if you look closely enough. I use medical language, and I interweave this with social and cultural understandings of disability poetics.

The reaction to the contrasts between how society observes disability, and how disabled or D/deaf people present their own experiences, is also important, and will be a major advantage in a disability poetics rooted in UK politics and history. Disability poetics allows us to reflect on the local and global history of disability rights; it also challenges how disability is interpreted in society today, and the current UK government's focus on disabled people as 'scroungers'. By foregrounding disability poetics as another way to present the experiences of disabled people, I believe we can have fruitful discussions on how disabled and D/deaf forms and styles of poetry can fuel a movement for social and cultural change in the UK and beyond. In my own work, I hope to use the influence of disability poetics to expand on the complexities of my personal experiences.

---

[17]   For a discussion about 'staring' from a disability perspective, see: Garland-Thomson, Rosemarie, *Staring: How We Look,* Oxford University Press, 2009.

Insufficiently Imagined: *Nuala Watt*
Partial Sight in Poetics

My practice takes partial sight as a philosophical and creative starting point. What is the role of partial sight in poetics? There are two main models. In the first, a blind or partially-sighted figure acts as an edifying spectacle for a sighted viewer. An example would be Edwin Morgan's poem, 'Blind'. The speaker sees a blind woman singing in the street and concludes:

> that when we see such fortitude,
> though she cannot, the day is good.[18]

The woman has no discernible features other than her visual impairment. She does not need any; her function is to provide a moral epiphany for the speaker. I dislike this poem. But it has galvanised my practice. I was so angry when I read it that I decided to talk back.

I wrote poems that foregrounded my experience as a partially-sighted person with cerebral palsy. I felt and still feel that there is a need to do this. My academic work focuses on contemporary poetry. I know and love many poems, but have read very few that present disability as a feature of a fulfilling life. The use of blindness as a totalising metaphor for incapacity has been so pervasive that to challenge it is a revolutionary act.

I believe that disability as a lived experience has been insufficiently imagined in literature. Literature reflects and influences society. So long as this imaginative failure continues, the profound inequalities that disabled people face in their everyday lives will go unchallenged, and perhaps even unnoticed, by the majority of the population.

These convictions place me, albeit uneasily, in the realm of identity poetics. In many of my poems there is relatively little difference between the speaker and the poet. 'I' is often me. There are clear advantages to a poetry of disability that foregrounds the

---

[18]   Morgan, Edwin, *Cathures,* Carcanet Press, 2002 (52).

self. Such a practice challenges previous portrayals of disabled people as little more than their impairment. My poem, 'On Her Partial Blindness', Is closely modelled on Milton's sonnet, 'On His Blindness[19]', presented here:

When I consider how my light is spent
    Ere half my days, in this dark world and wide,
    And that one talent which is death to hide
    Lodged with me useless, though my soul more bent
To serve therewith my Maker, and present
    My true account, lest he returning chide;
    'Doth God exact day-labor, light denied?'
    I fondly ask; but Patience to prevent
That murmur, soon replies, 'God doth not need
    Either man's work or his own gifts; who best
    Bear his mild yoke, they serve him best. His state
Is kingly. Thousands at his bidding speed
    And post o'er land and ocean without rest.
    They also serve who only stand and wait.'[20]

Milton struggles to come to terms with his impairment, and finally accepts it as part of God's plan. The sonnet is widely published; anyone who considers the poetics of partial sight in English must come to terms with it. I admire Milton's poem as a beautifully-crafted object, but I find its acquiescence disturbing. So I rewrote it using the same rhyme scheme and some of the same words. By closely following, but changing, the source text, I assert my right as a disabled woman to speak in the same tradition as Milton. He has a right to be in the canon. So do I. So do we.

To argue with canonical texts on blindness is very satisfying. But a poetics that stresses the disabled speaker's vision as a source

---

[19]   This poem is popularly referred to with this title, which was assigned by editor Thomas Newton in 1761, but the sonnet was originally called either '#16 'or '#19', and is sometimes referred to with its first line as the title.

[20]   Milton, J. (1673), *The Norton Anthology of Poetry*, Eds. Ferguson, Salter and Stallworthy, W.W. Norton, 2005 (418).

of truth runs the risk of reproducing the power dynamic that has historically objectified disabled figures in literature. It is just as possible for a disabled author to objectify a non-disabled figure in their poem as it is for the reverse to happen. I worry that this objectification may be present in my poem, 'Evangelist'. As a visibly disabled person I have had many difficult encounters with evangelical Christians who want to cure me; so, it was cathartic to write the poem. But I am concerned that just as the blind figure in Morgan's poem is there to create an epiphany, so the evangelist is there so that I can express my frustration. Both figures have been insufficiently imagined.

I would argue that a profound lack of imagination and empathy lies at the heart of the UK Government's current policies towards disabled people. Disabled people face a human rights crisis precipitated by welfare reform and cuts to social care. The United Nations produced a report on this topic in autumn 2016. My poem, 'The Department of Work and Pensions Assesses a Jade Fish', searches for an adequate creative response to a situation that often seems farcical and difficult to comprehend. In a world where people can die shortly after being declared fit for work, a DWP decision to assess a jade fish's medical problems would be no more nonsensical than most of their choices. Moreover, I wanted to explore the dehumanising nature of such assessments; in the 21st-century UK, a (truly beautiful) carving from ancient China can often be treated with more care than a disabled person.

Asserting personhood can be a key part of disability poetics. But it's not the only approach and can be unhelpful, especially in terms of the poetics of partial sight. Partial sight renders perception fluid and sometimes unreliable. To create a coherent narrative based on a single perspective can be misleading. It also fails to take into account the central role of partial sight in the composition of poetry. That is all poetry, whether it has explicit links to disability or not.

The most interesting parts of any poem are often those that the author did not see coming. There are clear links between partial sight and the partial apprehension that poets experience as they engage with an emerging poem. Writing to his brothers, Keats observed:

& at once it struck me what quality went to form a man of Achievement, especially in Literature & which Shakespeare possessed so enormously – I mean *Negative Capability,* that is, when Man is capable of being in uncertainties, Mysteries, doubts, without any irritable reaching after facts or reason – Coleridge for instance would let go by a fine isolated verisimilitude caught from the Penetralium of mystery, from being incapable of remaining content with half-knowledge.[21]

Partial sight, of necessity, obliges one to 'remain in uncertainties, Mysteries, doubts'. It insists on 'half-knowledge'. It is thus an excellent metaphor for the writing of poems. There is a second way of thinking about partial sight in poetics, one that is unconcerned with identity. Homer, the putative author of the *Iliad* and the *Odyssey,* is often presented as blind. Did Homer exist? If so, was he visually impaired? Does it matter?

I argue that Homer's blindness represents the limits of all human creative perception. Similarly, his explicit dependency on the Muse (both *The Iliad* and *The Odyssey* begin with invocations of this figure) represents poets' dependency on the volatility of language, on its unexpected turns. This positive portrayal of dependency in archaic texts runs counter to modern narratives. The toxic concept of 'welfare dependency' fuels the current human rights crisis. Our society places such a high value on autonomy that dependency is a frightening prospect for many people. Negative portrayals of disability in literature often spring from a fear of dependency and consequent lack of agency. For disabled poets, many of whom experience some degree of practical dependency, this view of poetics could be central. It shows partial sight and dependency as relevant to everyone who writes or reads poetry, regardless of their medical status. Disability is therefore not limited to identity poetics. It is a catalyst for all poetic activity.

---

[21]   Keats, John, 'Letter to George and Tom Keats [21 December 1817]', *John Keats: Selected Letters,* ed. R. Gittings, Oxford University Press, 2005 (41-42).

Dreams

The Body Politic

Rachael Boast

after Akhmatova

As if history tells itself this way: my country
not what it was, my city relatively at ease
with its decay. But what of the marks
on my body, skin falling in coded indices

of discord? I wear a parchment alphabet of grief.
Every movement ignites unnerved armies,
burns with enough friction to disturb
the border between one place

and another. Who will bear this pain
with me? It is not mine, not yours.
One day we'll finish cleaning the dust

from the feathers of nightingales and lift them
back to their rightful place –
for shouldn't they be always looking down on us?

🔊 bit.ly/saw46bodypolitic

141

Aubade

Rachael Boast

In the emollient night of roses and paraffin,
of burning hands and of all that burns

of broken sleep piecing together what for
so long had remained lost of what was lost

not in the dark but in the fire of the dark
in the night and in the oil of the night

of everything you were led to believe in,
everything stays secret until – one morning –

you put your hands through the touch
of the unfinished light and took it back.

🔊 bit.ly/saw47aubade

Lights of Silence   *Rachael Boast*

After the ordeal, I place a blade of grass
between my thumbs for a makeshift reed

until fish jump out of the darkness
and the circles in the river resemble laughter

whereupon my head breaks the surface
of the dream and touching the brightness

for a moment I see I'm covered in a gleam
of scales sleeping off staying awake

when the day should be night and the night
is too bright as the lights of silence –

ambassadors of the two worlds
I can't tell apart – loyal as they are

to one another tell me that the river
is the only true voice and the trees sing to it.

🔊   bit.ly/saw48lights

all that holds us   *Daniel Sluman*

once upon a time
you & i swam
from bed to bed
heavy with a hunger
for a love as light
as a bedsheet
to drown in

so much distance
& how far have we come ?

a middle-aged woman
with heavy eyes
peels off our socks
removing us
layer by layer
like she's fleecing cattle

the dry skin swirls
from my shin
& the waxy stripes
on my arms
won't be the first
she's ever seen

(a reminder
how deep
you can cleave
the flesh before
the body asks
the blood to swell

a reminder
of the gap
where all this
horror burns
between what
the body feels
& the mind demands
the body do about it)

she plies our skins
with emollient
thick as grease
& we are left to sit
in our sweat
like chops spitting
in the pan   this sofa
all that holds us
adrift   straying
further from the life
we were tethered to

in a pacific-blue hoodie
my fingers shake
around a thermos
as outside the guttering
chokes with ice
& the snow flurries
to fill roads like words
in a notebook

we wake
in the same room
somehow thinking
we're the same person
we were yesterday
in a world that feels
strangely familiar
strangely cold

the coffee we plunge
the cigarettes we roll
by the open window
the days disappear down our lips
& even sleep cannot carry
the weight of a human body
in distress   our dreams
felled   stacked & staining
the pillow like pollen

the carers come again
& again to unwrap us
of what holds us
until all that's left
are tears streaming
down tattooed wrists
& onto the sofa
that has carried us
like a mother
for eight months

a shallow grave
beneath a dusty ceiling
the lampshades lolling
like buoys through
the dark of so much
dumb slumber

*

do you ever wonder
where our bodies go
when we dream ?
how even in sleep
our hearts falter
& life cannot carry us
any further ?

the days pass
the room repeats us
inside it in endless variation
& how long would it take
for someone to notice
if we awoke or never broke
through the next morning ?

we are cripples
& death is what
we're meant to do
so long as we do it
quietly   so long
as we do it slow

🔊 bit.ly/saw49all

The View

Nuala Watt

Vision is still a draft.
The brain corrects the eye's syntax.

The trees are black lines, their roots seeking nutrients in blue earth.
The box on stilts will be a cathedral.

Those holes will become your face.
We walk on our hands over a deep blue ground.

🔊 bit.ly/saw50theview

The Department of Work and Pensions Assesses a Jade Fish *Nuala Watt*

Once, I held three thousand pale green years.

Should I compare myself to the jade fish?

I am in a museum of difficulties.
I feature in a national catalogue.
Handled, but not with care.

Juliet. Echo.
One. Five. Zero.
Treble Two.
C. That's me.

I'm a fraudster who walks.

Tick this box. Tick this box. Tick this box. Now.

How often do you lose consciousness?
Exactly how much of your life is a mess?

Can you make a cup of tea?

We cannot pay you.

The law says. The law says. The law says.
The phone squanders an hour.
This is because you have as much or more...

By the power of brown envelopes
I miss my class on poetics:
'Imagine The Voices of Things'.

On Her Partial Blindness
Nuala Watt

after John Milton

When I consider how to represent
my sixth of working light, my words collide
with your fear of dark. Your visions hide
the blindness born with me. You mourned sight sent
before you into death. Let me invent
a new account – half-light to place beside
your grief, the beauty of blind life denied.
I'd rather exploration than lament
sight as lost paradise. So my poems need
to make a sense I'm neither banned nor blessed
but breathing here. I want to have my state
revealed so thousands at my bidding read
as I eat, sleep, kiss, swear, get children dressed.
I feel and write. I do not stand and wait.

Evangelist

Nuala Watt

'Please will you let me pray for your feet?'
It's her third request this week.

If I believed, I would demand a warning.
I would ask God to mark this wet-eyed woman
a hazard on my route, like icy steps,
or that North Street blind corner.
'Yes', I smile. I can make her disappear.
But she stands gawping at my lace-up shoes.
I'm late for lunch, lurch past. 'Don't fret.
I'm off to see a friend.' But no one slipped
my happiness onto her mappa mundi.
I prowl on her world's edge like a bad dream.
So now I shut my eyes, letting her shape
a woman she'd prefer out of the air.

Receiving My Poems In Braille   *Nuala Watt*

My thoughts have arrived in the post.
I don't know which ones
I think they may be cyclists in the dark.

Nobody else touched sound,
so I shuddered away from the raised dots
that captured my name. Braille cells.

At playtime I was an empty space
among footballs. I stayed bilingual
for only minutes, afraid to be trapped

in a lonely alphabet.

Now silence arrives, enveloped. The dense paper
spins in my hands. Is it upside down?
Is this the love poem in which I'm a cobra?

My thoughts have arrived in the post.
I guess I'm somewhere, embossed.

Myoclonus   *Karen Hoy*

The lady concerned at my paleness
has touched my shoulder.

Legs kicking out from under me,
I slide down the deli counter

and from the floor, find myself
most Britishly apologising, again

like the time at the bus-stop;
the time in the supermarket;
the instance on the plane where
they gave me three seats to myself,
and the other passenger
just stared at my explanation
and brushed past me anyway.

Fear. Explanation. Doubt
of my explanation. Seizure.
That's how it happens.

But I'm not complaining.
This isn't to complain
it's to explain

how much I love to be held,
not tapped, poked, brushed by.
Held. I feel your body mop up
the electro-contamination.
You take it from me, politely,
like a heavy load I can't manage.

And I stay there, breathing in
the certainty, feeding on your stillness.

You earth my whole body
with a sentience of protons.

🔊 bit.ly/saw53myoclonus

Dr Ahmed's Ward Round　　　　*Karen Hoy*

...well they call it that,
but it's not, really.
It's a meeting

where the occupants
are summoned one by one
like an ark of singles.

This place... too old for access
to an outside space
like the new out-of-city

gardened units... too new
for affirmative architecture;
no high ceilings or kind kink

of picture rails and mouldings.
But hung with sun-faded still lifes;
vases of lilies gone overpastel

and wrong kind of blue
blue freesias – the distant blue
of neglected yesterdays;

the all-too-familiar colour
of the things in a back cupboard
of a cleaved mind.

And here, between patients,
the doctor almost forgets
to ask for any questions.

'Yes',

says the one leaving,
fully briefed on her medication,

'Where is the beauty?
Where is the beauty in this process?'

Mass   *Eleanor Ward*

Follow me into room four:
things are unsure but hopeful, the upper
hand is someone else's, not ours.
Four-hundred-kilo magnets
shine off your face, fixing where atoms
will fall. You talk about it with animation,
grab my hips as you point to every small
piece of the instrument, each pipe, foil.
Explain processes that I imagine: twirl, like us
on spring evenings. I wish I knew
more than the facts on my computer screen.
Science, the cerebral spinal fluid that might
be leaking out of my spine, the laxity
of my joints; clotting processes, how
blood falls when they meander lines up my arms.
You explain spectrometry one evening,
magic flashes into my mind.
You figure out the world's minute
properties, where small explosions
mean more than I can comprehend,
how light wiggles in mirages, off your face
my curious smile.

Structure

Eleanor Ward

The bruise on my knee has coloured itself
brown, purple lines and dots strike across it,
the sky at night I carry on my side.

Brief missteps, falling out of the bath, up
the stairs at the train station as commuters
climb over my back, step on my dress.

This failure to structure collagen correctly rips
my bones in and out of socket, no collagen
to buffer this crisp fall.

Watching the swelling, I carry my joints
upright, to my side, lift them above
my heart as I edge down concrete stairs.

Side Views

Eleanor Ward

If the helium is cut it will explode
he reassures.
I count out my MRIs on my fingers,

almost run out of hands.
I know the rules, remove everything
metal including projectiles,

bras just in case. I crackle the paper
on top of the moving table with my skin,
cold, goosebumped, my pelvis encased.

The only defence: ear defenders
press into bone jutting out below my ears.
Quickening beats start to delete the pop

playing underneath. I smooth the bell
they've handed me for emergencies,
until my hands slowly go numb.

Sudden shots shatter into lumbar spine.
I open each lid, rammed shut in defence,
to see black marks on white plastic.

I wait for a change in tempo, the end,
three centimetres away from
an encased plastic ceiling.

Walk out holding, grasp his hand,
find the beauty in the physics of the thing
I was pushed inside of.

The current switches,
hydrogen atoms are excited
while the magnets swirl,

away from all that fuss.

Old Scars

Julie McNamara

Rain falls harder
in empty places
beating on the hollow drum
of vacant hearts

Still clinging to the shabby walls
of the Albert Reynolds
the Essoldo
a perfect Palais
for the old Wirralians
of our misspent youth

We wake the wounds
over and over

And you want me
to step back with you
trace my fingers through the dust
carefully pick the cobwebs
from your matted hair

Join you
in this worried waltz,
scratching at old scars

🔊 bit.ly/saw54oldscars

Re-wired conversations: *Julie McNamara*
A very long career

I've worked with David Attenborough
Film or TV series?
I don't know

You'll have people round asking
They'll be wanting an interview
They will?

But I can't remember
I don't know what I've done
in my career…

It doesn't matter Mum
as long as you're happy

Am I happy?
Well you're smiling

That'll do then
Aye, that'll do…

Joodle?
Shirley?

Was it David Bellamy?
I think it's more likely
as you spend so much time in the garden

Does he like dogs?
He probably does

🔊 bit.ly/saw55rewired

Best Seat in the House   *Lisa Kelly*

my deafness	trumps	your male ego
your male ego	trumps	my television programme
my television programme	trumps	your reality show
your reality show	trumps	slobbing out
slobbing out	trumps	scoffing a family-sized bar
scoffing a family-sized bar	trumps	hiding a family-sized bar
hiding a family-sized bar	trumps	tearing up cushions
tearing up cushions	trumps	screaming and shouting
screaming and shouting	trumps	my deafness

🔊 bit.ly/saw56bestseat

Herring Loss   *Lisa Kelly*

Half heard, now half remembered
what was it I thought you said
as I beg my brain for the word I know
begins with *b*? The sense of something
on the tip of my tongue, which lurks
behind bottom teeth as lips purse *b*
goldfishing empty speech bubbles.

The Christmas cracker joke you told,
*What did the fish say when he swam
into a wall?* has an in-built sinker,
if not the right line, hooking *codswallop*,
all manner of red herrings, as I bang
my head against a brick wall, and hit
upon it was not *b* but *d. Damn!*

🔊 bit.ly/saw57herring

"Ellen McGrath Smith's essay in *Beauty is a Verb*, 'Hearing a Pear: The Poetry Reading on a New Frequency', helped me approach my mishearing as something that can generate different perceptions and understandings – generative creativity, word tag and word play being a crucial part of how I compose. Thinking about this and my personal experience of unilateral deafness through mumps in my left ear, I have chosen poems that best reflect how my 'half' deafness informs my poetic practice in terms of theme and aesthetics.

Because 'placement' and 'location' are so important to my hearing experience, 'Best Seat in the House' refers to this in theme and visually in relation to family dynamics. 'Herring Loss' uses the vehicle of a gag to explore hearing and memory loss, and reinforces my belief about the fun that can be had with generative creativity through alternative perceptions."

– Lisa Kelly

who needs olanzapine?

ploughshares beaten to rails to carry slate from fifteen hundred foot.
tunnel falls to hillside, arch-locking its origins, tooling where charge
wz placed. last nights northern lights to make yu weep: tag-games in
shadow pinks between saint sunday crag & hartsop dodd, ether blues
zag fairfield to stony cove pike, dreaming tangerine between high
street & dove crag. forget my antipsychotics this morning? who needs
olanzapine w/ patterdale at yr feet! this land is the roseate ov foxes
back broken on road below rough edge, the russet ov frosted brackens,
tarantellas ov rust on rails w/ nowhere to go. up here theyve beaten
ploughshares into, but beautifully

🔊) bit.ly/saw58whoneeds

166

Untitled

sean burn

from 'tattooing lorca'

one flew over the cuckoos nest
is all the staff training this one needs
you know how it is when they take against
this national front logo on obs corridor wall
and every time out my cell seeing that
needing a marker pen to cover it over
but they're all locked in the office
i ask, am ignored, instead
'medication', she orders
'meds rooms open now
later it will be closed'
and she steps in closer
fingers the red crash button
daring, staring me, i flex fists
feel 'em starting to pump
turn, punch out the wall
but still that nazi logo grins

🔊 bit.ly/saw59lorca

Impregnate

Naomi Woddis

This bauble of belly must be a mirage.
Is this what the angel meant
when he whispered, just out of range,
the mumble of the word *imp*?
One day it will be yours, a neat
rendering of a story, a page
scrambled with baby footprints, that one trip
worth more than the airfare. One magpie
means sorrow, two the joy you regain.
This boy's a magnet
and your heart's a metal-painter –
sky-shaped brushstrokes teaming
on steel. A brand new era.

Jagged

Naomi Woddis

Today I saw them both
in a photograph. Him
the new king, back
resting against
a hard-won throne.
Her face cross-hatched
with worry, wearing
pretty pink eye shadow
and a smile meant
only for pictures.
I still have the bouquet,
hardened to darkness,
its shadow jagged
as a dancer. Red
as the cry of first sex.

Maman

Naomi Woddis

In your 19th-century chateau
you watched your mother
weave her decline.
Your father's love for a governess
made a punch in you
to last a lifetime.

Your thick, small,
heavy, working hands
make legends,
tell the story
of nature in resin,
nails, twine and cloth.

Pink bandaged faces yell,
muted by stuffing.
A wooden totem is softened
by upholstery. Finally
you show us mother love
as the spider's eight-legged claw.

Like you
I cower under her,
tilt my child's face upwards,
motherward and afraid,
full of awe
and love.

Wandering Eyes   *Giles L. Turnbull*
after Helios

The world at the extremities of sight
is like a rainbow
superficially flat
a slight curl at the edges
a vain cut to the cloth
songbirds in attendance
keeping dust and fingerprints off;

after all the paths
and the mazes
each one bringing you back
to the world of local councils
obsessing over speed bumps and high hedges
because we like to know what's going on next door
behind the glass and the roses
after the pubs,
busy from midday to moon,
turn out at closing
with cold shoulder and a whiff of hops;

then, tiptoeing obliquely
the kiss of another morning
like the rainbow, reborn
high above rock and rubble
on the edges of the storm
in one house can be heard
somebody snoring
the sharp eye spies a man
shaving back stubble
a woman applying lipstick

before lifting the latch
to slip out as the world awakes,
the smell of bread freshly baked
and the fishermen bringing home the catch.

🔊 bit.ly/saw60wandering

Cold Hands *Giles L. Turnbull*

Feed me this dream. Feed me
whatever can purge me of this.
These drugs that I need, or so they say.
These drugs. I am not ill –
these drugs whose bottle my frail hand can't negotiate,
but whose administration I can't refuse. Leave aside.
These drugs which I need I don't need. I hate.
My frail hand won't reach out to take them from you. Take them from me.
Someone who can.
Witness a violent death happening slowly.
In the palm of my hand.
These drugs which I need. Take them.
These tranquilising drugs, which I need, take them. And give me my
frail hand back
time enough to open again.
Stop feeding me these potions and pills. These
drugs which I do not want. I do not need. I am not ill.

🔊 bit.ly/saw61coldhands

The Old Habits

Emily Ingram

Autumn blew tobacco in from the cold outside,
Carelessly distilled and bitter on the tongue.
She was like the sun; she was like a telephone
With men's baggy, frail words billowing behind her.

Seasons happened all at once, very early, that year;
Newspaper pennants trembled in the wind and ripped
And when the park laurels withered, we all wondered
If perhaps we should try to kick that old habit.

🔊 bit.ly/saw62habits

Paper Tanks   *Emily Ingram*

That year, the children made paper tanks for the dead
From frail Japanese sheets which folded and ripped
And didn't scream for mothers, or cost the school too much.

Like every year, they offered two minutes to think
And all the while wealthy men put paper in their suits
And sold guns to the countries Geography didn't teach.

Paper sheets red and flimsy on the cold stone steps
Of the merry chapel on the green, green hill
Where they laid the bodies who are lying there still.

They went home for Christmas, never thought of it again
And the tanks were recycled,
Though they threw away the men.

🔊 bit.ly/saw63papertanks

Medical illustration

Clare Hill

She scores red ink on her skin,
drawing from imagination
veins close to the surface.
Lungs like trees without leaves
are easy to sketch
but the pancreas proves tricky
and she's not sure about her spleen.
Heart beating faster, hand jumping,
she flat-lines the left ventricle.
The pen leaks itself dry.
Safety razors, blunt scissors,
useless ballpoint.
Cutlery drawer. Knife sharpener.

Brainfood

Clare Hill

split a piece of wood – you will find me

I turn myself inside out.
Examine fleshy packaging
for nutritional advice.
Reverse rice pudding skin
to reveal stewed liver and heart.
Create a red meat dress,
pull hands up through arms
leaving freckled gloves to dangle.

Replace eyeballs backwards.
Gaze at pickled walnut brains
where neurons dance the salsa.
Witness the miracle of digestion,
the last supper in glorious Technicolour.
Make sacred communion
with coconut biscuits and council pop.
Travel red veiny highways,
descend to marvel at a little toe.

God is in the details.

Careering Down the Hillside   *Catherine Edmunds*

He's a senior clinical psychologist, somewhere
a woman is singing; it is breaking him.
Stones scatter down the hillside as he runs,

he throws one hard, wrenching his shoulder.
Her voice is a ripple on the night, he is daytime,
solid and whole, he will not let her do this.

He kicks a tuft of grass, a toad squirms out,
limps away, he stares, horrified at
the dangling leg, wonders if he should

stamp out its life. He turned down promotion
in order to stay in this town, he told her,
she left. He reaches a stile, the knotted wood

consoles him, robust, smooth with the years.
He will never marry now. Death is an option,
but the chemistry of dying revolts him,

the seepage, the slow growth of toenails.
This day is too full of light. Celandines
open and glory in the sunshine. He grinds

them beneath his heel, curses the sky.
Next week, he'll wear a suit, attend meetings,
be quiet and kind, and his dreams will be smaller.

🔊 bit.ly/saw64careering

switness

Catherine Edmunds

a found poem

it has been possible to achieve
both the switness of sound
and the softness

one can recall the bowel strings of the past
but this type far better than the latter
owing to the promptness in emission

smooth bronze wound
cordes cuerdas corde armoniche
with sea-weed from the lagoon of Venice

🔊 bit.ly/saw65switness

What Is Possible   *Raymond Antrobus*

is that I will fly and I grow too big for my bed
like dreams have stretched me into a giant.
I cannot get enough sleep
because it is late, the TV is on downstairs
and I can hear it even though my hearing aids
are not in. I will complain about it
in the morning and mum will ask
why my hearing gets better at night.
It will take me another ten years
to appreciate how hard she has worked
to keep me warm in a house
it is true that I am held together by her love
but that string is buried too deep
inside me to pluck and say ah yes
I am only fully alive if you are.
I am in bed and there are stickers glowing
on the ceiling
so it is never completely dark
because I used to be afraid of it
but I have become friends with the dark
because it keeps me hidden
while I think about a girl I like who is not here
though I wish she was, we could do stuff
I don't yet know how to do.
It is possible I am going to wake up
a white American man like Tom Hanks
because I just saw the film *Big,*
I would do anything to dance
on giant piano keys playing 'Heart and Soul'.
It is possible that the only thing
that separates me from another universe
is the window I sleep next to.

It is possible that I know what is out there
and I can feel something inside my gut has legs
and is kicking saying, 'We can go anywhere
when we wake tomorrow morning.'
It is possible that I am just trying
to sleep inside myself and this
is the most peaceful sleep I will ever have.
The TV on downstairs while mum works
through the night threading jewellery
to sell at the weekend market. Sounds
muffle through floorboards,
my big sister in the bedroom upstairs.
I can't hear her but I know she is there –
she will wake up tomorrow morning
it is impossible that she won't.
It is possible I will fall
out of my skin and the dream will become
something I walk around in.

If All I Hear Is Your Gaze, *Raymond Antrobus*
My Body Won't Let Go Of Your Eyes

after Angel Nafis

*doesn't everyone lip-read I feel sorry for you do you sign or are you just
gesticulating why don't you have a deaf voice why do you need hearing aids
anyway when my ears pop I think of you I'm thinking about getting hearing aids
do they really work you're lucky to find it harder to hear women's voices
did you get the brown ones to match your tan at least if you grew
your hair no one will see them do you have to be so close to my face
forget it
I'm not repeating
myself*

🔊 bit.ly/saw66ifallihear

Dear Hearing World   *Raymond Antrobus*

after Danez Smith

I have left Earth in search of sounder orbits, a solar system where
the space between a star and a planet isn't empty. I have left a white
beard of noise in my place and many of you won't know the difference.
We are indeed the same volume, all of us eventually fade. I have left
Earth in search of an audible God. I do not trust the sound of yours.
You would not recognise my grandmother's *Hallelujah* if she had to
sign it, you would have made her sit on her hands and put a ruler
in her mouth as if measuring her distance from holy. Take your God
back, though his songs are beautiful, they are not loud enough. I want
the fate of Lazarus for every deaf school you've closed, every deaf
child whose confidence has gone to a silent grave, every BSL user
who has seen the annihilation of their language, I want these ghosts
to haunt your tongue-tied hands. I have left Earth, I am equal parts
sick of your 'oh, I'm hard of hearing too' just because you've been on
an airplane or suffered head colds. Your voice has always been the
loudest sound in a room. I call you out for refusing to acknowledge
sign language in classrooms, for assessing deaf students on what they
can't say instead of what they can, we did not ask to be a part of the
hearing world, I can't hear my joints crack but I can feel them. I am
sick of sounding out your rules – you tell me I breathe too loud, and
it's rude to make noise when I eat. Sent me to speech therapists, said I
was speaking a language of holes, I was pronouncing what I heard but
your judgment made my syllables disappear, your magic master trick
hearing world – drowning out the quiet, bursting all speech bubbles in
my graphic childhood, you are glad to benefit from audio supremacy,
I tried, hearing people, I tried to love you, but you laughed at my deaf
grammar, I used commas not full stops because everything I said kept
running away, I mulled over long paragraphs because I didn't know
what a 'natural break' sounded like, you erased what could have
always been poetry (strike that out). You erased what could have

always been poetry. You taught me I was inferior to standard
English expression, I was a broken speaker, you were never a broken
interpreter, taught me my speech was dry for someone who should
sound like they're under water. It took years to talk with a straight spine
and mute red marks on the coursework you assigned. Deaf voices
go missing like sound in space and I have left Earth to find them.

🔊 bit.ly/saw67dear

Legends

Their homecoming is not yet out of reach, not yet out of sight

Saradha Soobrayen

Sometimes I feel like a motherless child, a long way from home,
a long way from home...

The Archipelago is not where one man lived but is where
they all remember living. Remembering is like that.

Memory – a sliding door between adjoining rooms,
old and young Chagos hearts, co-habiting.

What were the last things you remember?
The man appears wide-eyed. Only four or five years old.

Every time he slides out a memory, a child slips back,
and boards the boat. The man considers what the child

knew then – the forced removal – the longing to return.
The Archipelago remembers him as a boy and each generation

is charged to remember the Archipelago. The past is tidal
in their minds or shall I say in their souls while the land waits

to recover the older selves, *tonton, tantinn, gran-per, gran-mer,*
a dying community, separated by unseen things, spirit from sea,

hope from land and yet united by wishful thinking, mouth
by mouth, their communal truths told in one continuous breath.

🔊 bit.ly/saw51home

'I will arise and go now, and go   *Saradha Soobrayen*
to Innisfree, and build a small cabin...'

Take comfort from Yeats' verse, *arise and go now, and go to* Diego Garcia
and *have some peace there*, and build a homestead not for one but for all

with Nature's blessing and insight. Confer with the Coconut Crabs
on the rising sea levels, listen to the last thoughts of the Hawksbill Turtle.

Conservationists cannot save what people do not cherish. If in doubt ask
the Chagos Brain Coral whose ancestral mind-fullness created the atoll –

collective thinking becoming land – propelling itself upwards,
an understated presence – however shy, the low-lying terrain is more

than able to express itself. Along the coastal reefs a murmuring
gathers strength; Shortfin Mako, Blue and Oceanic Whitetips,

shark replacements for the nuclear patrols safe-guarding
the open waters. All livelihoods rest on the responsibility to fish

a reliable catch; Dogtooth Tuna, Yellowfin, Bigeye, Albacore,
Indian Mackerel making its comeback in a surge of peaceful protest

in the shallows and in the depths in the streets and the high courts,
their homecoming is not yet out of sight, not yet out of reach.

🔊 bit.ly/saw52arise

They came, those that love like us. They came to marvel at all you had left behind – the glitter in your palms, the glam in your get up and go. They came in ones and twos with un-dry eyes, dahling boys biting their lips to stop from kissing you adieu one more time. In a tailored coffin that never grew into a perfect fit, you unwittingly became the burden of men too familiar with your scent. We walked behind clutching your box of fables, reaching for delivery – salvation you promised. They do not want us where you are going. So we measure every man by his weight in hydrated lime and in the inches of March rainfall; we capture thrown baited glances, lures into a mangled embrace. I'm sweet for the sway of winds without sorrow past our church door *by and by lord*. I seized your fading swirl as it slid up and under graveyard fissures around your fringed six-foot peat gown. We sang 'It's all right' to step ahead with arms around each others' cinched waists, awed at the tiny spaces between each dripping ghost for a thousand more of us. In comfort they came, those that love.

🔊 bit.ly/saw68longlive

189

Prometheus Baygrape   *Andra Simons*

i

Fire breathers, so the myth goes, with
doe eyes and men's ashen skin, are
born on isles too small to spot on the
colour-coded map of a breathless
empire,

born in a village of strange stones,
buoyant on a turbulent and limbless
ocean.

They lick at their wings preparing to
leap into the brittle and knotted grey-
haired sky, men who flare to mark the
passing of sunsets along the rows of
banana groves.

This is the stuff we recognise in the
opening chord of our tiny songs.

ii

Some men fear boys, the brave way
their cocks jump at the start. Big boys
with their flat chests, tar-black at the
twist of an arm, a frolic of thighs and
shoulders, tongues wagging. Mmmm,
bravado of hatching manhood.

I knew Prometheus Baygrape
walked these touchstone beaches,
near the guys who play ball with the
violent surf. But he dared to stand
where the ocean's white teeth rip at the
shore, the scent of blood carried to
high ground.

iii

When he set himself alight, such a
crackling brilliance, that aching
muffled bang, some thought him a
dragon, lighting other hearts aflame,

I feared most for him. Accident and
Emergency Units could only identify
him by the pattern of his teeth, each
crooked crown, each glow for help.

iv

I'm scarred by the one named
Baygrape. He left keloid moons on my
forearms when he reached for me
reluctantly.

I shhh his temper. I'm too old to
remember the lights.

Prometheus: combustible, brazen monk
blazing against this war and these
poverties.

I fear most for men born of that strange
glow. My carbon claws clutch at
setting embers.

Daughters

Andra Simons

Dead starlings, bizarre.
Mrs Knight's seven eye-
witnesses heard the impact.
The ground's instinct is to
swallow terrifying blood.
Dead starlings, beaks intact,
litter like lost footage of that
Hitchcock film. Omens dis-
played on a Sunday lawn.
The Royal Society for Fowl
admit there are odd things
in the universe. Dozens awaiting
results. All the Starlings are
waiting. Hardwired. Hundreds
nurse the frightened corpses. 53-
year-old expert baffled. Even in
Somerset they are beyond sleep.
Starlings once danced, now the
dead are adamant, they want
coordinated protection. They all
had flown, landed, curled in her
front garden (3.6 m long). Starlings
arrived out of the sky. Who would
have whispered onto the slipstream:
'Collide. Fall.'

The Girl with the Cold Sore   *Angela Readman*

She stacks spoons, one into the other,
silver hips that chase ice cream into streams,

balance cherries on sundaes, offer morsels
to wet tongues over tables. Here, love is

a red straw sucking cola, a coin in a hand
tapping the jukebox, itchy for a song

with words someone can sing. The busgirl hears
the sound of wanting all day, stashed in laughter,

kisses that gasp between tracks, airbeds of breath
full of slow punctures sighing to be fixed.

She pretends to be walking on sand, listening
to the oceans people pour into another's mouth.

If she stands still by the forks, she can imagine
seawalls, seeing a sparrow so close she may stroke it.

She holidays in smushes of strangers, soft smacks
of lips like birds learning calls beyond their nests.

The Love Machine   *Angela Readman*

Girls queue at the love machine, palms sweating
coins, profiles of queens paint our fingers green.

Between mallet and bell, where men ping their strength,
and the kissing booth, girls shuffle in a violet mist

of cologne, candy floss attracting wasps, lips glazed
to paint the scene of a kiss. One lass swings on the scales,

canary blonde, fingers crossed, legs pinched by forceps,
cheeks a pitted peach The Love Tester deems too ripe

to smooth the graft off a coalminer's neck. Another,
brunette, mutters I love you, I hate you before she steps up,

to sit on the scale a stone lighter, fly enough to love.
I kick off my boots, tie a balloon to my wrist, my parting

a towed line on my skull. I can't help but think of cock.
The love tester flashes pink as a can-can dancer splashing

a blush onto faces in the dark. Last, I place fingertips
into the iron glove of the slot and wait for the tape

to spool who my dirty, square fingered, hand fits.

The Invention of Velcro   *Angela Readman*

Later, he strolls to the house sniffing
the hands that gathered her perfume.

He shivers, still covered by the shadow
of the barn laying a suede blue cloth

on the grass where lad and lass
rolled into one for a heartbeat.

The bird eyes of blackberries oversee
the slow bow of summer, rupturing

his fingers. He pops a clot of October
in his mouth, sluices out the aftertaste

of her name on his tongue. For an hour,
at dusk he inspects his clothes, alone,

he makes a row of yellow leaves, twigs
and burr clover seeds stuck to his back,

picks at one blonde hair on his chest
like a crack he must carry wherever he goes.

Christina the Astonished   *Angela Readman*

The rafters are wormed with holes up close,
stars pinned to lost slates on the roof.

I assemble silence around myself like a church
and look down – sorry for my coat, ugly shoes
on the ground that can hold me no more.

The coffin is a doll's bed, so small I barely fit.
I soared out of it, lay my shadow on the casket
and tucked in my absence. I do not have to be

who I was. The women weep like watering mouths,
the curate hollows out grief simple as melons
relieved of their seeds. I look down, fissured

into the eyes of angels, licking breath turned
to water on stone faces in the eaves. I sip
in the sight of a woman carrying cornflowers.

In another life I could lift her into my arms,
be sorry, Mother, for bucking off ties on the bed,
stiff as a nightdress hung in the frost, but I'm not.

I couldn't help flying. She pushed my nose
to the floor so many times I finally learnt to miss.

"Officially, I don't have a disability (since ATOS occurred, I'm off the records), yet my condition disables me from a lot of work. I receive no income, yet have to, frustratingly, turn down most of the work I am offered. It all involves public readings of prose and poetry, and I have anxiety so severe I just can't do it. (Though I want to, need the income, and desperately want to get my work out there.)

Having anxiety is awful, not just because of the symptoms, but people's attitude to it. If I mention it to anyone, which I try not to, I am constantly met by comments like, 'Just do it', and 'Get over it', or, 'I used to be shy, work through it'. I hate having to explain it doesn't work like that. It has nothing to do with shyness, or not learning the skills to read in public (I worked on trying to get through it this way for years). Nor has it to do with always doubting my work.

One thing I have tried in the past few years, is trying to prove to people, and myself, that my poems aren't bad, hoping this would help the anxiety. I have won competitions, been commended, had work in journal after journal, but it hasn't made me able to read. It is difficult to approach poetry publishers, I am cautious because of the emphasis so many small presses place on readings.

Over the years, I haven't been able to find any support for my anxiety within the writing scene. I have wanted to quit, simply due to feeling ashamed trying to explain to people who don't understand. There seems to be an attitude around that if you can't read you don't deserve success. However, I have to write. The thing about anxiety is, it can lead to depression because of how utterly isolating it is. The only thing that prevents me being depressed sometimes is writing. Anxiety silences you, I open my mouth and the words won't come out, but when I write they can."

– Angela Readman

Our Hafren *Rosamund McCullain*

Following traditions of
The Thames, the Seine, the Ganges
Our Hafren divides the town.
On the other side, the lucky ones, resplendent
In their branded jogpants, faithful pedigrees
At their side.

No further than a spitted cherry pip,
Here on my side we are all muzzled mongrels
In backstreet counterfeits. Sink estates,
Beer-can bongs, the corpse of a baby rabbit,
Conversations as low-brow as our U-grade
Aspirations, the socially prescribed.

On a spring evening like this, Hafren,
She looks calm enough, oh yes.
But you just try to cross – she'll swallow you whole.

In addition to the patient information sheet

Michelle Green

to the steady beat
of a monthly script
she learns her lines by rote

not yet old enough to vote, but
perfectly poised at a junction of definition –
chemically swollen hips
wisped-away hair
the almost-death
of an almost-there sexual appetite
and blood-letting that comes
and goes
with military precision

a good little soldier
in the fight against deviance

she swallows the pill

following ten minutes of kind reassurance
from her doctor

she swallows the pill

back-pockets a leaflet about cancer risk
and ways to avoid impregnation

she swallows the pill

feeling grimly responsible
and grown up
and she is:

in all the ways she's expected to be
she is
flooded with synthetic estrogen
neck deep and still standing
she is
saturated
and safe

> *(and the boy in her holds his breath*
> *treads water opens his eyes then*
> *close blows bubbles from his nose to*
> *stay under stay under*
>
> > *stay)*

no uncomfortable threats
no
hunting
no
wanting for anything but
sanitised girl

no disruption
of the comfort of others of
rigid body norms of
binary two-step systems
and
is it normal
for a girl to have
such a deep voice?

no slip-ups
she is smooth
bleached
waxed
shaved

hetero-normally saved from herself
she is
stable
and
still

all stray strings of slippery queer
tucked safely away with
a once-a-day
orally administered
promise
to succeed
as a slowed
and sound-distorted
hormonally sedated
wait in line
till your given name
is called
sterile
seamless
female

🔊 http://bit.ly/saw69addition

About 4AM
Kitty Coles

The pull of the pills, at this hour, is palpable,
their sodden stupefactions, the sure, sweet numb.

They sing to me, imploring, 'Let us
guide you, ferry you under, hold you

down, good stones.' They taste of nothing
and they bring me to it. I fear the air's flavour

when I rise again, the rushing of wings,
the water in my lungs.

🔊 bit.ly/saw70about4am

A Gentleman and a Scholar   *Kitty Coles*

Tonight, you walk across my mind's surface,
in stockinged feet to keep the carpet clean
Your fingers drip ash like the fronds of a weeping willow.

In your flat, precarious towers
of books screen the walls floor to ceiling.
I perch on the sofa between two further mounds.

Diffidently, you exhibit the pot you made at the day centre,
round as a globe, with the lustrous smoothness of marbles.
You offer me raspberries, tasting of scent and summer.

You discourse on opera, the architecture of Rogers.
Your suit is faintly grubby at the edges.
When I bring up the past, you say you can't remember

your mind puncturing itself
like a pelican feeding its brood, revolving
in its own foxfire of suffering.

Five years since I saw you, you still
pad my memory's confines. You surface often,
haloed with smoke, old paper.

🔊 bit.ly/saw71gentleman

Migraine

Kitty Coles

The first warning: it begins
with borders thinning. Light
entering my pores, some substance
leaving.
I am smudging beyond
the boundaries of my body,
encircling it,
as ectoplasm, halo,
lipstick slipping
over the edge of the lip.

Submerged, I hear
boomily, speak in tongues.
There are acrid odours, unrecognisable.
I tell my hands to move. I'm amazed to see
them hopping, jerking,
marionettes, wild bunnies.

The walls are water,
swishing, falling, swaying.
Lights hover,
multitudinous spirits thrown from heaven,
towers sprouting,
ramparts shimmering,
the looming battlements of god.

Then the pain,
considerably less interesting.
It is bashing, insistent.
It swallows everything.

Afterwards, I am like a newborn.
I forget words for days.
I hold my breath, my head,
fearfully, stationary,
a balloon tugging its string,
a saucer brimming.

🔊 bit.ly/saw72migraine

Mercury   *Stephanie Conn*

1.

To be this close to the sun and still exist (orbiting
in your own eccentric way) albeit in extremes.
And us peering through lenses for your secrets,
while you halt; reverse, resume at speed.
What message do you bring from the gods?
Fry or freeze. What can you teach? What can you unleash
that won't be burnt to dust and blasted from the surface
by some solar wind? Your core – all depth, all density;
your outer shell, just that.

2.

Mercury, safely encased – the thermometer speaks;
her words are fluid and warn of water turning into ice
(or the risk of solids melting in the rising heat)
guarding carefully against the element of chance;
of being caught unawares on some freezing peak
wearing open-toed shoes, or languishing on desert sands
where nothing can live but poisonous, shrivelled, spiky things –
and the long-eared rabbits, the squirrels and the toads, the birds
and the willow, the poppies, the marigolds – vital, in the midday sun.

🔊 bit.ly/saw73mercury

View from a Rocking Chair   *Stephanie Conn*

after Edward Hopper's 'Room in Brooklyn', 1932

She sets the chair far enough back
to make the street disappear
so the windows frame rooftops.

The horizon is flat but for red-brick chimneys,
blunt against the blue expanse of cloudless sky.
She looks down nonetheless.

Fine black hair slips to skim her face,
exposes the curve of her neck,
naked flesh above the high-buttoned dress.

In a slant of afternoon light
five wooden slats keep her back straight,
the chair kept steady by her well-placed feet.

The table is out of reach. Its carved wood
covered by a plain blue cloth;
a porcelain vase placed carefully on top.

She loves its symmetry, a logical choice
for white roses that blush in the sun
and bend slightly towards the altered light.

🔊 bit.ly/saw74viewfrom

On the Astral

Colin Hambrook

young, I felt the breath
of a world that lives alongside
the everyday,

felt the crush,
a daddy long-legs
gasping to fly;

learnt to fight my way back
into the body, lying like a sack
on broken-down beds
of insect dreams,

no daily dose
of belladonna washed down
with a level playing field, could
take away those moments
of terror, wonderful

when the infinite
seems a bat's hair away
and sometimes I would ease
myself out of the body-grip
and find my essence able
to fly around the room

and out of the window, across
the night sky, like the times
with you – my eagle-love
chasing, the impossible essence
of you, flying the ether
far longer than your
material body could furnish.

🔊 bit.ly/saw75astral

Where the Sins of the Fathers Begin to Fade

Colin Hambrook

Down in the family machine, we mirror
each other like a moon in retrograde;
act on impulses determined by the bewildering chatter
of angels caught in the wings of an unconscious history.

I plan an empty horizon, keen to reach you
without triggering that razor blade feeling
that lodges in the pit of my stomach;
carries us back to where the beginning begins.

You throw glazed eyes at the wind
and I wonder if I can see what you see.
In your glance, catching the father's sins,
I melt into the ridiculous man with hands made of water.

We follow nature fooled by the belief
that the world can be turned; find insanity
under a bush of answers that move with the tide
of emotion; struggle and clay in the only place left to retreat.

🔊 bit.ly/saw76thesins

The Mirror That Refused To Look Back

Colin Hambrook

I had been hiding under the ironing board
in the kitchen, shelling peas neatly
into a Tupperware bowl;
pretending not to be,
when Mum's eternity blanket slipped,
revealing a Hall of Mirrors,
an endless parade of looking glass hallucinations
from the other side of Heaven.

Sleep never came easily;
interrupted by the nightly carnival,
playing in a dirty yellow light
at the top of the stairs
just outside the bedroom door:
a robber in striped jumper and eye mask
hovered with a bag marked 'swag',
big enough to take a whole life away.

And once, a lion with a full mane
lingered on the same spot,
at the foot of slumber,
threatening to roar the house awake.

Later, the visions came more subtly;
a mirror refusing the steady gaze
I offered its silvered surface.
Perhaps it couldn't embrace
the coating, like limescale
that grew from twilight reflections;
fractured, glowing, in the corners of the glass.

 bit.ly/saw77mirror

Dedication   *Colin Hambrook*

Words hang, limb-like, slip or crawl, insects struggling
to free themselves; lost in a mind-maze of endless corridors.
I work extra hard to retain a key to the store –
the bridges they create, the barriers they destroy.
Often invisible they hide, scuttling away in naughty corners
like children ready to trip for fun,
or resembling slug trails between me and you.

In the hardness of this word made flesh
I fall shy of reaching through this difficult veil,
lose you to urgent winds that blow the diagraphs to ash.
It isn't the content that counts, but whether it allows you in
to feel the quality of the chords' vibrations.

And facing the space between endings and beginnings
I look for you in the silence that holds the light
where words fall like tears; oxygen dissolving
in that briefest of moments, where life is.

 bit.ly/saw78dedication

211

"My poetry arises in response to distress. However, writing is not an act of therapy. Rather, it comes out of a necessity to explain myself in a world that makes little sense. I cherish words and find release in the images that arrive at my door through the portal of experience. I was incubated in the sterile light of psychiatric diagnosis; in part, my writing comes from anger at the injustice of the labels that the mental health profession lays upon people whose experience doesn't fit the mould of 'normality'. It seems to me that psychiatry makes a pact with the devil, in the sense that it chooses to give reductive and facile explanations that work in contradistinction to our shared humanity. I dedicate this selection in memory of Kraean with whom I shared a struggle against a childhood of religious oppression and psychiatry."

– Colin Hambrook

Pinderfields, 1968 *Lydia Popowich*

Flat on a bed in C.C.U.
Through the bay window, a December view
up high, the Burns Unit, tidy red bricks, wet roofs,
one naked tree in billowing skies.
Flat on my nine-year-old face. I see
close-ups, starched linen landscapes,
browse pillow stories of wrinkled roads,
nowhere hills and valleys.
Rough peaks and dark ravines
cut cryptic signs in perfect skin.
Crimson rivers unravel my punctured wrist.
I twist, that way, this way
to see the tree
and *Nil by Mouth* taped to iron railings
while dust and paint shavings
tally time
and the clock on the wall clings
forever to five to five.
Property of the NHS, my mouth
is a desert storm. In the morning
soft shoes slip-slapping on linoleum,
nurses giggle, shuffle behind trolleys of tea,
dispensing cornflakes and potions of sweet opium.
At night, they play cards under a desk lamp
while the old lady moans
slumped in her chair, without a blanket.
I twist, that way,
this way to see.

🔊 bit.ly/saw79pinderfields

Leeds, 1976   *Lydia Popowich*

The ambulance man with striking
green eyes stroked the inside
skin of her teenage arm as she lay
strapped (for her own safety) on the reeking
canvas of another NHS.
'If you're a lucky girl you will meet Jimmy!'

She thought he was, maybe,
trying to be nice (but those alien
fingers were electric...) No comfort
blanket, suspended in L35, skeletal
traction, legs akimbo and knicker
-less (for her own hygiene), a monster pain
-ted by Hieronymus Bosch. The male charge
nurse with watery grey eyes brought gin
secrets in a Barr's Cream Soda bottle, hot
take-away through her open
window of gritty nights.
She thought he was, maybe,
trying to be nice (but gin made her sick,
she liked Babycham).

'The glass half
-full on the sunny side.
Cheer up, might never happen',
said the porter with the lizard pink
eyes, taking her down to a strip
-lit basement, down corridors
lined with conduits.
'If you're a lucky girl you will meet Jimmy!'

🔊 bit.ly/saw80leeds

Alice in Check

Joanne Limburg

The bedroom is a battle scene, Alice at one end,
her mother at the other; two queens on a chessboard.

Alice is outnumbered, but she holds her own,
because she fields the Knight Whose Name Is NO!

and boldly he has snicker-snacked his bloody way
straight through her mother's forces. See them on the floor:

the Choking-Collar-Dress, the Orange-Flower-Yucky-Taste,
the Frilly-Dot-Bow-Monster. They want to make Alice

into a girl for looking at, stop her tongue
and force her skin to scream. They should be vanquished,

and would be, if Alice were allowed to win, but not today.
Her mother does the worst thing she could ever do:

'Now look – you've made your Mummy cry!'
The Knight Whose Name is NO! shakes his wet head

and Alice, who must save them all from being drowned,
gives up, and lets herself be dressed for looking at.

🔊 bit.ly/saw81alicecheck

The Alice Case   *Joanne Limburg*

'The problem with Alice', the Caterpillar says,
      'is her rigidity of thought.'

'Yes', says Humpty Dumpty,
      'and her lack of empathy.'

'Indeed', says the Caterpillar.
      'Her mind-blindness.'

'Yes', says Humpty Dumpty.
      'Her inability to read faces.'

'Indeed', says the Caterpillar.
      'Or tone of voice.'

'And then', says Humpty Dumpty,
      'there's the flatness of her affect.'

'Alongside', says the Caterpillar,
      'the strangeness of her prosody.'

'As well as', says Humpty Dumpty,
      'her adherence to routine.'

'Not forgetting', says the Caterpillar,
      'her repetitive behaviours.'

'Or her failure', says Humpty Dumpty
      'to understand a joke.'

'Or her lack', says the Caterpillar,
　　　'of any feel for metaphor.'

'Or her inability', says Humpty Dumpty,
　　　'to hold a proper conversation,,,'

'Excuse me', says Alice,
　　　'may I say something?'

'Of course', says the Caterpillar,
　　　'you may say something – '

'Yes', says Humpty Dumpty,
　　　'and we'll tell you why it's wrong.'

🔊 bit.ly/saw82alicecase

The Mermaid   *Markie Burnhope*

The care regimen of a broken Siren,
offspring of the ocean dried to a crater,
cripple-daughter of a desert father:

Tailfin feet fanned out left and right,
the shimmer of cream on dry-scale skin
after a long soak in lukewarm water.

My thighs not fused, but so heavy to lift
from bath to towel they may as well be, and this
monstrous mass entirely cursed with fur

because I lack the mobility or the stamina
to contort myself into the shapes to shave,
let alone hold those poses for long enough.

Man. I imagine snapping his mast
not between my thighs but in the gaze
of my eyes. Myriam offers a hand

on with the rest of my clothes
and a whole ship is crushed in the call
of one of my names.

🔊 bit.ly/saw83themermaid

Toomsday Device   *Markie Burnhope*

There were times I took my crutches
onto the escalator, stared down
at the steps, and imagined a man's blood
escaping from beneath the gaps.
Yes. I improvised a Southern Gothic sermon
in my mind: it is written
the hour will begin when a slender un-man
emerges from their nest,
its architecture packed with agony columns,
brutal letters to editors, butterfly-spreads
of disparate flesh parts like Rorschach marks.
Yes. After two-hundred years' hibernation
inside the walls of the best big-box retailers
they will come out, to seek the nourishment
of gen-Xers' livers, to rejuvenate the shine
of their yellow-green eyes, the calcium
of their foldaway bones.
Yes. Maybe this game made it easier
to handle my shaky-cam frame,
distract myself from the nervousness that rose
the closer I came to the ground,
the whiplash that happens when metal returns
to mall-floor surface, and a cripple can trip
and fall. No. I was neither predator nor prey
in this scenario, less proximal, more parallel
to man and woman. Made to watch them
attend their days more from hospital beds
and carpets of healing conferences
than my own two feet. No. I did not know
non-binary, but I knew Spina Bifida; had felt,
with a finger, the groove in my natal cleft.

Knew, too young, the reality of my identity
being reduced, erased, hence why I glanced,
whenever the chance arose
not into windows and doors for clues
but shafts, grates, vents, places where elements
go from one state to the next: air to wind, blood
to food; culture their best,
least burdensome selves.
When given no place to stand
we tend to revert to crawlspace. Yes.
Capitalist cult television, a machine to lower me
down into oblivion, let me – with a glee
allowed one who for now responds to 'boy' – snap
that fleeting morsel of promise from its palms. No.
I was eleven, of course
I never murdered a man. Yes. I was an accomplice.

🔊)) bit.ly/saw84toomsday

The Eves Were Us

Markie Burnhope

Our narratives not of girls – we were
no one's sisters or daughters – but girls made
monsters of weeks, raised as bane
of fathers, wolves and women
and taken, two by two, by guardians
who parked us not behind bars
but motorway services,
cutting the radio DJ off at the point
when, between quick spits of static:
'Controversy is rising over the effects
of aspartame on our children, a misleadingly
potent poison, experts say –'
and told us: 'Wait in the car or come'
into the petrol station
to buy syrupy cola, stretch our legs,
use the restroom, before hitting the road again
to wherever they were taking us,
whispering their problem from the front
as we went: how to tether two tearaway
effectively-female imaginations to reality,
tell the difference between bluebells
and foxglove, hunt down a pair of handcuffs
friendly enough – soft, pink, fluffy enough –
that we might consent to wear them
for the duration of our interrogation,
bearing twenty unrotten rows of teeth between us.

🔊 bit.ly/saw85theeves

On the Final Days Before Your Transformation

Markie Burnhope

for the sixteen year-old lycanthrope, Marie, and her late mother

May you mystify dentists
with your teething.

May your exposure to the politics of body hair
be a slow-burn
and the snatches of time spent
undeniably girl, feel like surrounding yourself
with a microfibre towel.

May you find pleasure in texture, pattern, colour,
for as long as humanly possible.

May you be gaslit no more
than the once I saw. Compliant – if you want –
only in the sense of medicated, otherwise
finding ever-inventive ways to antagonise doctors
convinced they'd already lived the red scare.

I don't care. Let them camp out in a tent
and document the sounds of our womanhood.

I don't know what your mother would have wanted,
only, let me put my face up close to the metal
of her empty wheelchair, in the hope
I see my reflection there.
Please.

This is important. I have an investment,
a need to see you living well for a while.

🔊 bit.ly/saw86finaldays

Descriptive Text of Photos and Vispo (Visual Poetry)

🔊 bit.ly/saw87descript

Cover

The picture serving as backdrop to this book's cover, the back cover as well as the front, is 'Tate Modern Extension, 2015' by co-editor Khairani Barokka, a photograph taken of a section of Tate Modern then under construction. It shows colourful zigzags of scaffolding in overlapping geometric patterns. As an unfinished structure (of an arts institution, no less), its inconsistencies exposed, it might symbolise and parallel the insufficient, incoherent societal structures underpinning and attempting to undermine our lives as D/deaf and/or disabled people and artists. Taken another way, it shows the beauty of structures and bodies deemed by society to be 'unfinished', which are already whole in their/our own right.

Front Cover

The front cover says: 'Stairs and Whispers: D/deaf and Disabled Poets Write Back / Edited by Sandra Alland, Khairani Barokka and Daniel Sluman'. 'Stairs and Whispers' is written in a staggered layout, mimicking stairs. The font is white, with the i's of Stairs and Whispers in yellow, as well as the forward slashes in 'D/deaf' and between the title and the editors' names. In the lower right-hand corner are the name, 'Nine Arches Press', and its logo (an arch over a crossed symbol), in white.

Back Cover

Against the same backdrop as the front cover is a semi-transparent white rectangle, on which is written the following text in black:

Stairs and Whispers: D/deaf and Disabled Poets Write Back, edited by Sandra Alland, Khairani Barokka and Daniel Sluman, is a ground-breaking anthology examining UK disabled and D/deaf poetics. Packed with fierce poetry, essays, photos and links to accessible online videos and audio recordings, it showcases a diversity of opinions and survival strategies for an ableist world. With contributions that span Vispo to Surrealism, and range from hard-hitting political commentary to intimate lyrical pieces, these poets refuse to perform or inspire according to tired, old narratives.

"This is a collection which redefines what poetry is. This is a collection which is nearly as varied as the diversity of impairment and disability and D/deaf experiences in Britain today. This is a collection which I will read and re-read until I have absorbed the richness and colour and anger and misery and humour and power of it." – Tom Shakespeare, author, *Disability Rights and Wrongs*

"The face of next-generation disability poetics announces itself with a roar – razor-fine lyric, body knowledge, crip humour and revolutionary grief are all on display, along with something more: the joy of the discovered self. The poems here are gorgeous and important." – Sheila Black, co-editor, *Beauty is a Verb*

"*Stairs and Whispers* is an incredible addition to crip literature that I'm excited to add to my shelf! The poems and essays featured here are at once devastating, enraging, and uproarious for me as a queer neurodivergent writer of colour." – Lydia X. Z. Brown, activist, writer and speaker

"Watching the new surge of Deaf poets take on the world of BSL, film and creative captioning feels very important ... to reclaim the right to be a poet and to use both signed and written word to demonstrate the diversity and richness of the Deaf community ... commenting on being Deaf, politics of identity and a celebration of who we are." – Jenny Sealey, Artistic Director, Graeae Theatre

Below this rectangle, from left-hand corner to right-hand corner, the following appears in white: the logo and name of Nine Arches Press, the words 'Cover artwork', the copyright symbol (a 'c' in a circle), then 'Khairani Barokka'.

The barcode of the book, above which is written: 'Price: £14.99, NAP065, ISBN: 9781911027195'.

Spine
Against the dark burgundy background of the book's spine is the following text: 'STAIRS AND WHISPERS: D/deaf and Disabled Poets Write Back' (in white), 'Eds. Alland, Barokka & Sluman' (in yellow), and 'Nine Arches Press' (in white).

'Doublespeak' (Visual Poem), Abi Palmer, p.38

Abi Palmer writes, 'The image is a found poem from a sheet which accidentally went through my printer twice. It should be noted that one side contains an extract from my medical records, written by Dr Simon J Newell on 16 June 2010.' The image contains this extract, right-side up, and also the accidental fragment of another document, upside down, on the lower portion of the page.

The first text reads: 'Abigail has suffered injury to her corpus striatum. It is possible that this injury occurred at some time around delivery. It is not however clear that earlier delivery would have avoided this. 5 Delivery of Abigail's head was more difficult than is often the case. Her body was delivered through the uterine incision. Her mother then watched her body go blue before the consultant arrived. The consultant extended the incision in the uterus and this allowed delivery. 10 The reasons for this are explained the expert in obstetrics. One not uncommonly sees the fetus delivered by breech Caesarean section where there is difficulty with delivering the head. In very difficult circumstances, the fetus may suffer injury due to APA. In these infants however, one expects delivery in a poor condition so that resuscitation is 15 required. The infant will become unwell and need admission to the baby unit. Characteristically if injury has occurred there is a neonatal encephalopathy. It is therefore my view prior to multidisciplinary discussion, that it is 20 unlikely that delivery without the difficulty in delivering Abigail's head, could have altered the outcome.'

The second text says: 'Onlookers observe the "black blood", "corrupted blood", along with "blood untainted" / As father and husband stain the streets, carrying the bleeding body through Rome / In this case staining of caused by lucrece's powerless loss of virginity is its own trigger into further darkness. - relationship between play and the poems'.

'The Unforgotten, or Mary do you want to talk about last night' (Visual Poem), Sandra Alland, p.97

The image is an x-ray from below the neck to the pelvis; of note are the uneven hips, the curved and compressed spine, and a circular piece of jewellery in the stomach region.

The following text is spread over the x-ray in yellow font: It's gone now. The smell. Used it all up I guess. That's the problem with depression isn't it: robbed of a second interview, lots of pro bono. I'm not sure how much you children know about pagers, but no marriage is perfect is it. Don't nudge my arm. What I want to know is do I define fertile the same as you. I don't suppose brothel is an option on the form.

'Tin Eaters', Aaron Williamson (Visual Poems), pp.98-100
Each 'poem' in 'Tin Eaters' was made while concentrating for one hour on the tinnitus Williamson has learned to ignore.

'Tin Eaters #1', p.98
Williamson places an artful composition of numerical and linguistic symbols and fragmented imagery, of different textures and shapes, colliding and complimenting each other, in a black square frame against a tan backdrop. The number 40, a road sign of a car on a dock, a bright red pattern with a star, a brick wall.

'Tin Eaters #7', p.99
A series of letters and geometric images in black, gold and red – the sign for nuclear hazard, dots, arrows, curves, an asterisk, the number three, the words 'thoughout the world' upside-down – tumble together and apart in an unexpected composition, framed by a black rectangle on a tan page.

'Tin Eaters #14', p.100
A black square on a tan page houses black letters and geometric images placed at whimsical angles to each other. Juxtaposed, varied font sizes spell out 'splice', and letters spill from one end of a curved arrow to the other. Blue, radiating rays are in the upper right-hand corner of this square. Also the word 'total' and repeating Ns and Rs.

'Long Lost Lover' (Film Still by Ania Urbanowska), Bea Webster, p.119
This close-up image is of poet, Bea Webster. She is Scottish-Thai with a septum nose piercing and shoulder-length dark brown hair pulled back into a pony-tail. Bea is signing the British Sign Language for 'tree' directly into the camera, and looking gently at her hands. Close

together at the wrists and held out in front of her, her hands have all ten fingers spread out in the shape of branches.

'Turtlemen: Bishop in Love' (Film Still by João Trindade), Andra Simons, p.120

The image is of a shirtless black person, visible from just below the shoulders, wearing blue sparkly earrings and a white head scarf. In front of and obscuring their chest are the person's hands, holding a large glass jar filled with cloudy water. They look into the jar, laughing.

'The Stars are the Map' (Film Still by Kyra Pollitt), Gary Austin Quinn, p.121

The image is of poet, Gary Austin Quinn, a white man with short, light-brown hair. He wears a long-sleeved purple shirt, and stands in front of a bright blue background, framed from the chest up. Gary is performing the poem in British Sign Language – his hands are in the air mid-movement. Above him are the words, 'stars are the' in white, with a white drawing of a constellation also visible. At the bottom of the screen are orange captions in Shetlandic: 'Da starns is da map I unrowl.'

'Bilingual Poet's Dilemma' (Film Still by Ania Urbanowska), Donna Williams, p.122

The image is of poet, Donna Williams, a white woman with short brown hair. She wears a black button-down shirt with three-quarter sleeves, rectangular black glasses and hearing aids with blue moulds. Standing in front of a white background, Donna is framed from the waist up. She is making the BSL sign for 'how', and looking at her hands as if to say, 'How do I do this?' The words 'match, match, match' appear around her in a playful yellow font, and at the bottom of the screen the captions read 'How to make it rhyme?'.

'Am I Mentally Ill or Am I Just a Dickhead?' (Film Still by Mattr Media), Jackie Hagan, p.123

The image is of Jackie Hagan, a white poet with shoulder-length rainbow-coloured hair, blue eye shadow and tattooed arms. Jackie is wearing a green cardigan, multiple colourful scarves and shiny gold trousers. She is sitting in the second of four rows of orange theatre or cinema seats. To her left are a pair of crutches. Jackie looks into the camera while gesturing towards herself, perhaps as if to say, 'Who, me?'

'Goat Poem (for the kids)' (Film Still by Mark Mace Smith and Anigman), Mark Mace Smith, p.124

The image is of a dirt road in Majorca, with green grass and leafless shrubbery on either side. The road leads off into the fog. On the left side of the road is a goat. Along the road and facing away from the camera are three versions of the same figure – wearing all black. The closest version of the figure stands facing slightly to the left, and the other two walk away from the camera along the road. The middle version of the figure is accompanied, on the right-hand side, by a second goat (which is actually the same goat). The words 'by all means necessary' appear in white font over the centre of the image.

'The Sword Swallower' (Film Still by Ania Urbanowska), Markie Burnhope, p.126

The black and white image is of a woman in silhouette behind a screen, framed from the hips up. She stands facing right with her head tilted back and mouth open wide. She holds a crutch above her head with both hands as if preparing to swallow it. A second crutch hangs from her left arm, perpendicular to her body and with the handle facing away from her at a right angle. The silhouette contains sharp detail, including curly hair, a pair of glasses, a skirt, and the outline of the woman's teeth.

'Stare' (Film Still by Leonore Schick), Miss Jacqui, p.127

The image is of a live performance by Miss Jacqui, a black woman with black and burgundy medium-sized dread locks. She is sitting facing the left side of the screen, looking upwards and smiling. Miss Jacqui wears a black shirt and has a piercing in her visible left ear. On the screen in white font are the words 'Miss Jacqui, Spoken Word Artist'.

'Kettle's Boiling' (Film Still by Sandra Alland), Alison Smith, p.128

The image is of poet, Alison Smith, a white woman with short red hair and red lipstick. She is outside standing in front of a tree, and there are leafless trees in the background. Alison is in the right side of the frame, framed from the nose down to just above the shoulders. She's wearing a grey jacket with a fake fur collar, a grey and black striped scarf and a bright pink dress. Alison is signing in British Sign Language with her left hand, and the caption reads: 'Can't you lip read?'

Content Notes

We know it's impossible to know and therefore to list what warrants a content note for everybody, but we've done our best to try to list topics some people may wish to know about before reading, below.

Reclamation of Ableist Terms
- 'shove ten pounds of sugar in a seven pound bag', Daniel Sluman, p.19
- 'Nothing About Us Without Us, No One Left Behind', Sandra Alland (essay), p.24
- 'A Language We Both Know', Raymond Antrobus (essay), p.105
- 'No Body to Write With: Intrusion as a Manifesto for D/deaf and/or Disabled Writers', Abi Palmer (essay), p.107
- 'Am I Mentally Ill or Am I Just a Dickhead?', Jackie Hagan (film), p.123
- 'How can we identify a UK disability poetics?', Eleanor Ward (essay), p.129
- 'all that holds us', Daniel Sluman, p.144
- 'The Mermaid', Markie Burnhope, p. 218
- 'Toomsday Device', Markie Burnhope, p.219
- 'Some Short Definitions for Complex Ideas', p.238
- Thank Yous, p.259

Descriptions of Ableism and/or anti-Deaf sentiment
- 'On Living Our Poetries', Khairani Barokka (essay), p.16
- 'Nothing About Us Without Us, No One Left Behind', Sandra Alland (essay), p.24
- 'Help Wanted', Holly Magill, p.47
- 'What Can You See?', Holly Magill, p.48
- quote from Abigail Penny, p.54
- quote from Raisa Kabir, p.60
- 'Wash Your Hands Before You Leave Toilet', Cath Nichols, p.65
- quote from Georgi Gill, p.74
- 'dlrow', Sarah Golightley, p.77
- 'CV Template, Disability 2.0', Sarah Golightley, p.80
- quote from Gram Joel Davies, p.84
- quote from Cathy Bryant, p.94

State Violence (from medical professionals, schools, police, DWP, ATOS, etc.)

- 'Prometheus Baygrape', Andra Simons, p.190
- 'Daughters', Andra Simons, p.192
- 'Christina the Astonished', Angela Readman, p.196
- 'Toomsday Device', Markie Burnhope, p.219

Sexual Violence
- 'this body has not', Claire Cunningham, p.39
- 'Goat Poem (for the kids)', Mark Mace Smith (film), p. 124
- 'Leeds, 1976', Lydia Popowich, p.214

Descriptions of Racism or Colonial Violence
- 'On Living Our Poetries', Khairani Barokka (essay), p.16
- 'Nothing About Us Without Us, No One Left Behind', Sandra Alland (essay), p.24
- quote from Raisa Kabir, p.60
- 'A Language We Both Know', Raymond Antrobus (essay), p.105
- 'Long Lost Lover', Bea Webster (film), p.119
- 'Goat Poem (for the kids)', Mark Mace Smith (film), p.124
- 'Untitled', sean burn, p.167
- 'Their homecoming is not yet out of reach, not yet out of sight', Saradha Soobrayen, p.187
- 'I will arise and go now, and go to Innisfree, and build a small cabin...', Saradha Soobrayen, p.188

Descriptions of Heterosexism
- 'Long Lost Lover', Bea Webster (film), p.119
- 'Kettle's Boiling', Alison Smith (film), p.128
- 'Long Live the Queen', Andra Simons, p.189

Descriptions of Cissexism, Transmisogyny and/or Forced Gender Conformity
- 'On Living Our Poetries', Khairani Barokka (essay), p.16
- 'Nothing About Us Without Us, No One Left Behind', Sandra Alland (essay), p.24
- 'No Body to Write With: Intrusion as a Manifesto for D/deaf and/or Disabled Writers', Abi Palmer (essay), p.107
- 'In addition to the patient information sheet', Michelle Green, p.199

- 'Alice in Check', Joanne Limburg, p.215
- 'The Mermaid', Markie Burnhope, p. 218
- 'Toomsday Device', Markie Burnhope, p.219
- 'The Eves Were Us', Markie Burnhope, p.221
- 'On the Final Days Before Your Transformation', Markie Burnhope, p.222

Descriptions of Classism
- 'Nothing About Us Without Us, No One Left Behind', Sandra Alland (essay), p.24
- 'No Body to Write With: Intrusion as a Manifesto for D/deaf and/or Disabled Writers', Abi Palmer (essay), p.107
- 'Our Hafren', Rosamund McCullain, p.198

Sexual Imagery
- 'Circus', Cathy Bryant, p.90
- 'No Body to Write With: Intrusion as a Manifesto for D/deaf and/or Disabled Writers', Abi Palmer (essay), p.107
- 'Turtlemen: Bishop in Love', Andra Simons (film), p.120
- 'Jagged', Naomi Woddis, p.169
- 'Prometheus Baygrape', Andra Simons, p.190
- 'The Love Machine', Angela Readman, p.194

Strong Language
- 'she's punctuation she's', Abi Palmer, p.37
- 'dlrow', Sarah Golightley, p.77
- 'CV Template, Disability 2.0', Sarah Golightley, p.80
- 'Audience', Sandra Alland, p.95
- 'No Body to Write With: Intrusion as a Manifesto for D/deaf and/or Disabled Writers', Abi Palmer (essay), p.107
- 'Am I Mentally Ill or Am I Just a Dickhead?', Jackie Hagan (film), p.123
- 'Goat Poem (for the kids)', Mark Mace Smith (film), p.124

Dead or Injured Animals
- 'Circus', Cathy Bryant, p.90
- 'Careering Down the Hillside', Catherine Edmunds, p.178
- 'Daughters', Andra Simons, p.192
- 'Our Hafren', Rosamund McCullain, p.198

Some Short Definitions for Complex Ideas

Sandra Alland with
Khairani Barokka

(that we encourage you to read more about from
people who have spent years researching and theorising)

Friendly reminder: When it comes to using disability terms, self-identification is imperative. Please don't label people without their permission.

Disability According to the UK's Social Model:

In 'the social model of disability', first developed into specific disability theory and activism in the UK in the 1970s and 80s[22], people are 'disabled by society, and barriers are created by external socio-cultural structures and the physical environment'[23]. For example, the problem is not one's inability to walk; it's the lack of lifts, step-free access and money for good assistive devices. This way of thinking is in opposition to the medical model, 'which places onus on an individual's impairments as the source of barriers'[24].

Disabled Vs. Person-First and Difference Language:

In the UK, where ideas around the social model have led or influenced most disability activism, it's most popular for people to self-identify with the term 'disabled people' – as opposed to using 'person-first' language such as 'people with disabilities', or alternative labels such as 'differently abled[25]' or 'functionally diverse'[26]. Person-first language lists the word 'person', then the word 'with', then the person's impairment or identity.

For some people, this is merely a difference of vocabulary or cultural reference point, while for others each of these kinds of terms

---

[22]   Slorach, Roddy, *A Very Capitalist Condition: A history and politics of disability,* Bookmarks, 2016 (19).

[23]   Lawrence, Matson, *Barriers to Access: Report on the barriers faced by young disabled and D/deaf people in accessing youth arts provision in Scotland,* Birds of Paradise Theatre Company, 2016 (7).

[24]   Ibid.

[25]   This term is mostly used in the United States and Canada.

[26]   This term originated in, and is mostly used in, Spain.

might be considered offensive or harmful. While there are individuals or communities that prefer person-first language, many disabled people in the UK and US have come to reject it on the basis that it suggests particular impairments or identities are negative. While the stated intention is to emphasise the person and not the condition, the negative associations of 'person with' often remain similar to 'suffers from', and insinuate an unwanted burden. When we use 'Autistic person', instead of 'person with autism', writes activist Lydia Brown: '...we recognise the value and worth of that individual *as* an Autistic person.'[27]

Likewise, language such as 'differently abled', though attempting to address that impairment doesn't equal un-able, is often criticised for failing to acknowledge the barriers disabled people face – and for suggesting (in arguably infantilising language) that there is 'one normal way to be human'.[28] Again, self-identification is what's important, and non-disabled people might consider refraining from arguing an issue that does not directly affect them.

D/deaf:

The term 'D/deaf' (capitalised 'D' followed by a slash and then a small 'd') is an umbrella term for numerous identities within D/deaf communities. A small 'd' is generally used to denote the audiological 'condition' of deafness, and most often applies to those who might also use terms like 'deafened' or 'hard of hearing' to describe themselves. For many people, Deaf (capitalised 'D') specifies a distinct culture and language – in the UK this is most often rooted in British Sign Language (BSL). Because of this cultural foundation, Deaf is often regarded as a category distinct from disability. However, there is some overlap with the social model of disability, as 'D/deaf people also face barriers within mainstream

---

[27]   Brown, Lydia X.Z., 'The Significance of Semantics: Person-First Language: Why It Matters', August 4, 2011, accessed April 12, 2017. http://www.autistichoya.com/2011/08/significance-of-semantics-person-first.html

[28]   Brown, Lydia X.Z., 'How "Differently Abled" Marginalizes Disabled People', August 29, 2013, accessed April 12, 2017. http://www.autistichoya.com/2013/08/differently-abled.html

hearing-centric culture and society'[29], such as lack of provision of captions, speech-to-text services, lip speakers and BSL interpreters.

Mental Distress, Mad Pride, Neurodiversity:

There are a variety of experiences that the umbrella term 'disabled' attempts to encapsulate, but communities and individuals may prefer other, more specific terms. Many mental health communities, or individuals in mental distress, might not use 'disabled' to describe themselves, but instead (or additionally) choose 'mad', 'mental health survivor', 'in mental distress', or the name of a specific mental health diagnosis or condition. Reasons can include a desire for specificity, a shared history of unique oppression, and that certain forms of mental distress are less easily 'enabled' by changes to physical and social environments.

The term 'neurodiversity' includes learning disabilities, specific learning difficulties/differences like ADHD and dyslexia, dyspraxia, Autism, and other neurological differences.[30] People from these groups might use 'neurodivergent', 'neurodiverse', 'Autistic person', 'Aspie', 'dyslexic' and/or other terms for themselves, sometimes in order to emphasise a unique identity or history of oppression. Neurodiverse people, a group that can include people in mental distress, may also have connections to the social model; they can face barriers within mainstream culture and society, arguably not rooted in having an 'impairment', but instead in not being properly accommodated. Again, self-identification is key.

Illness and Chronic Pain:

People who experience severe illness and/or long-term chronic pain also might not use the term 'disabled', or might not (fully) ascribe to the social model. Like with mental distress, such conditions are not always easily 'enabled' by changes to physical and social environments.

---

[29]   Lawrence, Matson, *Barriers to Access: Report on the barriers faced by young disabled and D/deaf people in accessing youth arts provision in Scotland*, Birds of Paradise Theatre Company, 2016 (7).

[30]   Slorach, Roddy, *A Very Capitalist Condition: A history and politics of disability,* Bookmarks, 2016, (212-218).

240

Crip Culture:

The term 'crip' has origins in United States disability activism, and some parallels with words like 'queer' in terms of reclamation and re-definition of language. Similar to historical reclamations of queer, crip can espouse radical politics in direct opposition to mainstream ideologies around the integration of people from a marginalised community into the normalising ableist mainstream[31] (which is also white supremacist, classist, heterosexist, cissexist and misogynist). The queer movement and queer theory set themselves up in opposition to the corporatisation of Pride, and to middle-class, rights-oriented fights like gay people in the army and equal marriage. Similarly, crip culture resists the idea of disabled people trying to access and blend into the oppressive mainstream. For some people, this term is still contentious because of its historic use for harm.

Beyond (White) UK, European and US Perspectives...

This anthology aims to include various disability cultures, and the decolonisation of disability and crip studies to include non-white experiences of disablement and a keen acknowledgment of intersectionality. Experiences and meanings of disability vary greatly across history and place, and ideas being explored in modern-day UK have been examined in myriad ways across the centuries. For example, Javanese notions of disability as spiritually important were denied by colonial Dutch doctors and medical institutions – who sought to 'cure' disability at all costs[32]. In this sense, Javanese disability history is predicated on a social model, but one that predates UK work on social models entirely, reaching back hundreds of years into Javanese culture. And that's just one example.

---

[31] McRuer, Robert, *Crip Theory: Cultural Signs of Queerness and Disability,* New York University Press, 2006.

[32] Thohari, Slamet, *Disability In Java: Contesting Conceptions of Disability In Javanese Society after the Suharto Regime,* 2013.

Biographies and Notes

Aaron Williamson is inspired by his experience of becoming deaf and by a politicised yet humorous sensibility towards disability. Williamson devises unique artworks that are created on-site immediately prior to their public presentation. In the last ten years he has created over 300 performances, videos, installations and publications in Europe, Asia, Australia and North America. In a 1998 talk at University of California San Diego, Williamson coined the term 'Deaf Gain' as a counter-emphasis to 'hearing loss'. http://www.aaronwilliamson.org

'Could It Just Be' is an excerpt from 'Chimp Jus', a series of poems created for the Stephen Cripps Bursary Award and to be published later this year by a small press in Oxford. The concrete or vis poems are part of another series Aaron created on the bursary, 'Tin Eaters'. Each 'poem' was made while concentrating for one hour on the tinnitus he has learned to ignore. The original pages toured the US with an exhibition Aaron curated for the Bluecoat, Liverpool: 'Art of the Lived Experiment'. 'Tin Eaters' scanned images appear courtesy of Kendall College of Art and Design of Ferris State University.

Abi Palmer is an interdisciplinary writer and artist. Her interactive poetry project *Alchemy* was voted 'Best Wildcard' at the Saboteur Literary Awards 2016. Recently she began working with mycologist, Nathan Smith, to create *Mycolyrica*, a project aiming to develop new poetic forms influenced by the structure and reproductive patterns of fungi (mycolyrica.tumblr.com). Abi's 'top terms' have included Psoriatic Arthritis, Ehlers Danlos Syndrome and 'Mild Cerebral Palsy'. www. abipalmer.com @abipalmer_bot

'Body Language' is composed from wording collected from various physiotherapists during rehabilitation sessions. 'Doublespeak' is a found poem formed from a sheet of paper that went through Abi's printer twice; it contains an image of her medical notes by Dr Simon J Newell on 16 June 2010. 'Government Body' was previously published on *Fit To Work: Poets Against Atos*. 'She's punctuation she's' was previously published on thispace blog. 'Voter in Blue' was previously published in *Rising.*

Abigail Penny: My name is Abigail Penny, I am 25 years old and I have recently graduated from the University of Gloucestershire with a degree in English Literature and Creative Writing. Since my infancy I have had problems with social interaction, and when I was 16 I was formally diagnosed with High Functioning Autism. Because of my difficulties with social interaction, my interests include solitary pursuits such as writing poetry and going on long country walks.

Alec Finlay has published over forty books; recent publications include *Global Oracle* (2014) and *I Hear Her Cry* (2015). Finlay has had M.E. since 1990. He has also composed poems and artworks reflecting on illness and healing, including commissions for Beatson West of Scotland Cancer Centre, Glasgow, and creating the National Memorial to Organ and Tissue Donors, at the Royal Botanic Garden Edinburgh, opened in 2015. www.alecfinlay.com Some of this material appeared previously in the journal, *Bibliotherapy*.

Alison Smith: I'm a Deaf, queer, BSL performance poet from the Scottish Showpeople community. My writing and performing draws on personal experiences and life's observations. Since 2009 I have been using film as a medium, performing in 'Fingers' and creating 'Kettle's Boiling' (in collaboration with Sandra Alland). When I perform I prefer to have voice-over by another artist.

'Kettle's Boiling', part of the online extension of this book, has been part of several festivals and exhibits, including Entzaubert (Berlin), LGBT History Month Scotland and Disability Arts Online's Viewfinder.

Andra Simons is an award-winning Bermudian writer, director and actor residing in London. His poems and plays have been published and performed widely in Canada, Bermuda and the UK. https://andrasimons.wordpress.com/

'Long Live the Queen' was previously published in *Bermuda Anthology of Poetry II*. 'Turtlemen: Bishop in Love', made in collaboration with João Trindade, is part of the online extension of this book, and has featured at events including Who's Your Dandy? (Edinburgh Filmhouse).

Angela Readman's poems have won The Mslexia Poetry Competition, The Charles Causley, and The Essex Poetry Prize. They have been published in journals including *The Rialto, Magma, Ambit* and *Popshot*. She also writes stories, and is a twice-shortlisted winner of The Costa Short Story Award. Her story collection, *Don't Try This at Home*, won a Saboteur Award in 2015. Her latest poetry collection is *The Book of Tides* (Nine Arches Press, 2016).

Ania Urbanowska is a Polish-born filmmaker based in Scotland. She creates fictional, experimental and documentary films. She also collaborates with international artists on A/V performances and cross-platform projects. Ania has directed several short films that engage with subjects including the power of subconscious and coincidence, fear and sexuality. Most recently she collaborated with Sandra Alland on the multidisciplinary performance, 'Equivalence' (Transpose/Barbican and Anatomy), and edited an award-winning short documentary, 'Where We Are Now'.

Ania collaborated with Sandra Alland to create three film-poems for the online extension of this book: Bea Webster's 'Long Lost Lover', Donna Williams' 'Bilingual Poet's Dilemma' and Markie Burnhope's 'The Sword Swallower'.

Bea Webster is a mixed raced queer woman who wears a cochlear implant, living in Glasgow. She currently studies BA Performance in BSL and English at the Royal Conservatoire of Scotland. She has a big love for anything creative, especially the theatre arts.

'Long Lost Lover', made in collaboration with Sandra Alland and Ania Urbanowska, is part of the online extension of this book.

Cath Nichols teaches creative writing at Leeds University. Pamphlets are *Distance* (2012) and *Tales of Boy Nancy* (2005); full-length collections are *My Glamorous Assistant* (2007) and *This is Not a Stunt* (2017). She wrote a feature for Mslexia on Writing and Disability – after critiquing ableist advice in their 2015 Diary. She has a Creative Writing Pedagogy and Disability chapter in *Avoidance in the Academy* (2015, Routledge) and another on Trans* and Disability in

Trans* and Female Masculinities (2015, Cambridge Scholars).

'Accommodation', 'Wash your hands before you leave toilet', and 'Migration of the Brown-Grey Unicorn *Leptonycteris yerbabuenae'* will appear in *This is Not a Stunt* (Valley Press, 2017).

Catherine Edmunds was educated at Dartington College of Arts and Goldsmith's College, London. After twenty years as a musician, she re-invented herself as an artist and writer after becoming disabled. Her published written works include a poetry collection, four novels with Circaidy Gregory Press, and a Holocaust memoir. Catherine has twice been nominated for a Pushcart Prize and three times shortlisted for the Bridport. She has also been published by *The Frogmore Papers, Butchers' Dog* and *Ambit.*

Cathy Bryant worked as a life model, civil servant and childminder before becoming a professional writer. She has won 25 literary awards and her work has appeared in over 250 publications. Cathy's published books are: *Contains Strong Language and Scenes of a Sexual Nature, Look at All the Women*, and *How to Win Writing Competitions (and make money)*. Cathy is bisexual, and mentally and physically disabled. See Cathy's monthly listings for cash-strapped writers at www.compsandcalls.com

Note on 'Ms Bryant is Dangerously Delusional': This poem is made from statements said or written about me and/or my partner, Keir. People assumed that I was on benefits, but I wasn't at the time these statements were made. However, I believe strongly that people should be treated with respect whether or not they are on benefits, which most people claim only when they absolutely have to.

Christine de Luca is a native Shetlander, living in Edinburgh. She is currently the Edinburgh Makar (poet laureate), and interested in Scotland's languages. She writes: 'This collaboration was a joy, bringing to life the story of an amazing single-handed voyage. So many skills had to be fused together to achieve the beautiful end result.' Christine is the author of the English and Shetlandic poems, 'The Stars are the Map' and 'Da Starns is Da Map'.

'The Stars are the Map', made in collaboration between Gary Austin Quinn, Kyra Pollitt and Christine de Luca, is part of the online extension of this book (video with BSL and English/Shetlandic captions, and separate Shetlandic and English voice recordings by Christine de Luca).

Claire Cunningham is a self-identifying disabled artist/performer/ choreographer based in Glasgow, Scotland. Cunningham's work, while rooted in movement, often features text or song. Her physical vocabulary comes from the study and use/misuse of her crutches, and the exploration of the potential of her own specific physicality with a conscious rejection of traditional dance techniques (developed for non-disabled bodies). Her texts are all extracts from her performances. www.clairecunningham.co.uk

'First contact' is from *Under the Radar* (2007) by Jess Curtis/Gravity, text by Claire Cunningham. 'This body has not' is from *The Way You Look (at me) Tonight* (2016) by Claire Cunningham & Jess Curtis, text by Claire Cunningham.

Clare Hill has an impressive collection of sparkly walking canes alongside many pairs of heels she can't walk in but refuses to throw out. With work published in magazines such as *Raw Edge, Trespass, adc* (art disability culture), *Twisted Tongue* and various anthologies, she is currently hoping to be a writer in the 1980s so she can avoid both social media and people in general. However, she does, albeit grudgingly, maintain a blog at https://painchick.wordpress.com.

Colin Hambrook has a background as an artist/survivor of the mental health system, arts facilitator, and disability arts journalist. He is author of two illustrated poetry collections: *100 Houses* (DaDaSouth, 2011) and *Knitting Time* (Waterloo Press, 2013). He has 20 years' experience working at the hub of the Disability Arts Movement as an editor/producer, publishing and showcasing work by disabled artists, fostering networks and enabling debates around the development of disability arts practice.

Daniel Sluman is a 30-year-old poet and disability rights activist. He co-edited the award-winning disability anthology, *Fit To Work: Poets against Atos*, and was named one of Huffington Post's Top 5 British Poets to Watch in 2015. His second collection, *the terrible*, was published by Nine Arches Press last year, and he is currently preparing for a PhD at Birmingham City University.

'Shove ten pounds of sugar in a seven pound bag' previously appeared on *Fit To Work: Poets Against ATOS*. 'All that holds us' will appear in *Well Versed*.

Debjani Chatterjee MBE has been called a 'national treasure' (Barry Tebb). She has worked in industry, teaching, community relations and arts psychotherapy. An acclaimed international poet, children's writer, translator, cancer survivor, Olympic torchbearer and storyteller; she chaired the National Association of Writers in Education and was Poet-in-Residence at Sheffield Children's Hospital. She is an Associate Royal Literary Fellow and Patron of Survivors' Poetry. Her 65+ books include: *Namaskar: New and Selected Poems.* More at www. dchatterjeewriter.simplesite.com

'What I Did Today' was originally published in *Do You Hear the Storm Sing?* (Core Publications, 2014), and appears on Disability Arts Online.

Donna Williams is a Deaf poet who uses English and British Sign Language. Working with such different languages has inspired a deep interest in translation and how her work can be made accessible to both hearing and D/deaf audiences. She has performed at poetry festivals around the UK as well as in America and Brazil, and has appeared at the Edinburgh Fringe. Her poems cover many themes, from bilingualism to identity, to her beloved cats.

'Bilingual Poet's Dilemma', made in collaboration with Sandra Alland and Ania Urbanowska, is part of the online extension of this book.

El Clarke is a poet and writer of short and flash fiction, based in Kent. She writes about the beauty and destruction she sees in the world around her, and about personal interactions. She lives with her cat,

Willow. When not writing she reads, crafts and plays roller derby. She also happens to be gay and have Ehlers-Danlos Syndrome, and believes there should be more in the literary world for young queer people.

Eleanor Ward is currently a PhD student in Creative Writing at The University of Manchester. Her thesis concerns the cultural model of disability, gender and identity in contemporary poetry about disability, and these topics inform her creative work. Eleanor has been writing for over 15 years and enjoys the challenge of how to represent disability in poetry.

Emily Ingram: Originally from Portsmouth, Emily (also inexplicably known as Molly) is a writer, director, and stage manager living in Edinburgh with ME/CFS and a small cat called Gremlin. At the age of 15, she was diagnosed with dyslexia, dyspraxia and other specific learning difficulties. Around the same time, she also discovered that poetry was much more interesting than most other things and started trying to write it herself. It proved addictive.

'The Old Habits' was previously published in *Freak Circus* (Issue 1, Autumn 2015).

Gary Austin Quinn is Assistant Professor leading BSL within Languages and Intercultural Studies at Heriot-Watt University, Edinburgh. A profoundly Deaf life-long BSL user, he became interested in the arts in 2004. In 2007 he established *Visual Virus*, creating BSL performances for Deaf and hearing audiences and staging two performance pieces at the Edinburgh Fringe 2012: *Through New Eyes* and *Dream or Not*. He is the author of the BSL poem, 'The Stars are the Map'.

'The Stars are the Map', made in collaboration between Gary Austin Quinn, Kyra Pollitt and Christine de Luca, is part of the online extension of this book (video with BSL and English/Shetlandic captions, and separate Shetlandic and English voice recordings by Christine de Luca).

Georgi Gill writes and works in Edinburgh where she lives with her wife. She is studying for an MA in Creative Writing at Manchester Metropolitan University. Diagnosed with multiple sclerosis thirteen years ago, Georgi is interested in exploring how we use language to define and describe illness. Her poetry has been published in *Far Off Places*, *The Interpreter's House*, *Dactyl* and *Gutter*, and was featured in the anthology *A New Manchester Alphabet: An Illustrated Collection of New Poetry 2015*.

'A drawn out magic trick' was first published in *The Interpreter's House* #59, 2015.

Giles L. Turnbull has been writing poetry for 25 years, and every day he loves how it reveals things that he had not heard or thought about in the same way before. He lost his sight nine years ago and is still finding curious ways in which the changes to his perception of the world emerge in his writing.

'Wandering Eyes' was first published in the pamphlet *Dressing Up* (Cinnamon Press, 2017.)

Gram Joel Davies lives in Devon. His recent poetry may be found in *The Interpreter's House*, *The Fenland Reed* and *Dark Mountain*. His diagnosis with a mood disorder simply put a name to his sense of having been born into the wrong world. Too often, he finds that unseen disability is met with disbelief. Find him online at:
http://gramjoeldavies.uk

'I Am Hive' was previously published in *Lighthouse Literary Journal,* and was shortlisted for the Wells Literature Festival Poetry Competition 2015 and the Plough Arts Centre Poetry Prize 2016. 'Creep' was previously published in *Well Versed (The Morning Star)*. 'I Am Hive' and 'Creep' are also in Gram's collection, *Bolt Down This Earth* (V. Press, 2017).

Grant Tarbard is the former editor of *The Screech Owl*, co-founder of Resurgant Press, a reviewer, and an editorial assistant for *Three Drops From A Cauldron*. Previously, he was the first runner-up (at the age of sixteen) in Ottakar's/Faber National Poetry Competition. He is the author of *As I Was Pulled Under the Earth* (Lapwing Publications),*Yellow Wolf* (Writing Knights Press) and *Loneliness is the Machine that Drives the World* (Platypus Press).

'When Under Sodium Pentothal' was previously published in the pamphlet *Loneliness is the Machine That Drives the World* (Platypus Press, 2015). 'Vascular Graft' will be included in *Rosary of Ghosts* (Indigo Dreams), forthcoming this year.

Holly Magill is from Worcestershire. She has a BA in Creative Writing from the University Of Birmingham and has had poems in various publications, including *Bare Fiction, Morning Star, Clear Poetry* and *The Emma Press Anthology of Mildly Erotic Verse*. She co-edits *Atrium* (www.atriumpoetry.com) and is on the reading panel for *Three Drops from a Cauldron's* seasonal specials. She is visually impaired since birth.

Isha has written poetry since childhood and for many years was a regular emcee and stand-up poetry performer and facilitator for Survivors' Poetry. She has had poetry published in several anthologies, including *Under the Asylum Tree* (Survivors' Press), *From Lead to Gold* (Survivors' Press) and *In Protest –150 Poems for Human Rights* (The Human Rights Consortium). She has also taught poetry writing and performance. She identifies as a mental health survivor, physically disabled and marginalised.

'Pieces' was previously published in *Fit to Work: Poets Against Atos*.

Jackie Hagan is a multi award-winning queer amputee who enjoys talking to people about class and art. She is a committed community arts worker and inspiring workshop facilitator, specialising in working with 'difficult' people. She recently represented the UK at an international poetry slam in the favelas in Rio, and was the focus of a Channel 4 documentary.

'Am I Mentally Ill or Am I Just a Dickhead?' was published in *Asylum* magazine and *Some People Have Too Many Legs* (Flapjack Press, 2015). The film version, by Mattr Media, is part of the online extension of this book.

Jacqueline Pemberton: I have written short stories and poetry for many years. I completed an MA in Creative Writing and set up a local writers' group that was successful in encouraging new and experienced writers.

I originate from Suffolk although I have lived in the Northwest for many years. I have had rheumatoid arthritis for 27 years, and retired from teaching three years ago through ill health. I published a collection of my poetry last year. I lead a happy and active life.

'Body Polish' was previously published in *Aware: Edition 11* (Chorley and District Writers' Association magazine). It also won the Local prize in the Southport Writers group competition in 2016.

Joanne Limburg: I've published two other collections: *Femenismo* (2000) and *Paraphernalia* (2007). *Femenismo* was shortlisted for the Forward Prize for Best First Collection and *Paraphernalia* was a Poetry Book Society Recommendation. Other poetry publications include *Bookside Down* and *The Oxygen Man*. *The Woman Who Thought Too Much,* a memoir about OCD, was published by Atlantic in 2010. My novel, *A Want of Kindness*, appeared in 2015, and a second memoir, *Small Pieces: A Book of Lamentations,* is forthcoming in 2017.

'Alice in Check' and 'The Alice Case' are from a series called 'The Autistic Alice', and appear in Joanne's most recent collection from Bloodaxe, also titled *The Autistic Alice*.

Julie McNamara: I am a London-based, Liverpool Irish playwright, poet and performer. I'm a mad woman made good and an outspoken activist in Disability Arts. My work springs from dark places, from landscapes of madness and sheer mischief. I'm driven by a passion for social justice with a yearning for re-connection to human kindness. The safety of the voyages provided by the written word give me freedom to explore my darkest desires and obsessive ruminations.

'Re-wired conversations: A very long career' appears as a scene in the stage play, *Let Me Stay*, co-created with Shirley McNamara.

Karen Hoy: Born in Newport, Wales, Karen had a full-time career in international television before developing ME. She also has, or doesn't have, epilepsy, according to whom you ask, and whether they think it is good for her to know it. Karen now lives in Wiltshire working part-time. Her work has been published in journals and anthologies, and she has a Diploma in Creative Writing from the University of Bristol. Karen blogs at reasonablyadjustedtv.com.

'Dr Ahmed's Ward Round' came 9th in the 2015 International Welsh Poetry Competition, and is downloadable from the winners list webpage. The poem also appears in the Welsh Poetry Competition Anthology 2012-2016, *Ten Years On*, edited by Dave Lewis and published in December 2016.

Khairani Barokka is a writer, poet, artist, and PhD researcher at Goldsmiths in Visual Cultures. Published and working internationally, she is the writer/performer/producer of *Eve and Mary Are Having Coffee*, co-editor of *HEAT: A Southeast Asian Urban Anthology* (Buku Fixi, 2016), writer-illustrator of *Indigenous Species* (Tilted Axis, 2016), and author of *Rope* (Nine Arches, 2017). In 2014, UNFPA recognised her as an Indonesian Young Leader Driving Social Change.
http://khairanibarokka.com

Kitty Coles lives in Surrey and works as a senior adviser for a charity supporting disabled people. She has been writing since she was a child and her poems have been widely published. She is one of two winners of the Indigo Dreams Pamphlet Prize 2016, and her debut pamphlet, *Seal Wife,* will be published in August 2017. www.kittyrcoles.com

'A Gentleman And A Scholar' was previously published in *Brittle Star* and 'Migraine' in *South.*

Kuli Kohli: I am a creative writer, poet, mother, wife and full-time council worker. I was born with mild cerebral palsy. I'm a dedicated member and co-coordinator of Blakenhall Writers' Group in Wolverhampton. Writing has opened up all sorts of possibilities as I struggle to express myself through speech. Having the ability to write has made my life richer. I write a regular blog for Disability Arts Online. My debut poetry collection, *Patchwork*, was published by Offa's Press in 2016.

'Equilibrium' appears in an earlier form online at Offa's Press.

Kyra Pollitt is a translator, poet, and artist, with a PhD on poetry in natural sign languages. As Artist-in-Residence at the Scottish Poetry Library, Kyra conceived, facilitated, curated and produced the collaborative piece 'The Stars are the Map'.

'The Stars are the Map', made in collaboration between Gary Austin Quinn, Kyra Pollitt and Christine de Luca, is part of the online extension of this book (video with BSL and English/Shetlandic captions, and separate Shetlandic and English voice recordings by Christine de Luca).

Lisa Kelly is deaf in her left ear from childhood mumps. She is half English and half Danish. She trained and worked as an actress and is now a freelance journalist living in London. Her pamphlet *Bloodhound* is published by Hearing Eye and she regularly hosts poetry evenings at the Torriano Meeting House in London. She is a board member of *Magma Poetry* and has an MA in Creative Writing from Lancaster University.

'Herring Loss' was previously published in *Antiphon* Issue 17.

Lydia Popowich is a writer based in Caithness, Scotland. Disability, alienation and body fascism are themes underlying her work. She was a founding member of Northern Disability Arts Forum in Newcastle during the 90s. Her poems have appeared in anthologies and magazines including *Dream Catcher, Northwords Now,* and *Obsessed with Pipework*. Her first pamphlet, *The Jellyfish Society*, was published in 2016 by Paper Swans Press. She uses fragmentation as a metaphor for disability.

Mark Mace Smith: 'Culturally disabled' by being born Black in 1970s London, Mark Mace Smith chose art and Manchester as his escape from the pitiful pre-prescribed condition of the young black Briton whose options statistically leant towards prison, 'lunatic asylum' or McJob. Through poetry, acting, music, painting and photography, Mark has explored all elements of the arts for some financial recompense balanced within a lifetime of freedom from a 9to5 or institutionalised servitude. Mark makes Art. Mark is happy.

'Goat Poem (for the kids)', made in collaboration with Anigman, is part of the online extension of this book.

Markie Burnhope was born in Oxford in 1982, with Spina bifida and Hydrocephalus. She now lives in Bournemouth with her wife and stepchildren. Her debut poetry collection, *Species*, was published in 2014 by Nine Arches Press.

'The Sword Swallower', made in collaboration with Sandra Alland and Ania Urbanowska, is part of the online extension of this book.

Michelle Green is a British-Canadian writer and spoken word artist. Her short stories have appeared on Radio 4, in *Short Fiction Journal*, and on the interactive story-mapping app *LitNav*, among other places. Her poetry chapbook *Knee High Affairs* was published by Crocus Books, and her debut collection of short fiction, *Jebel Marra* (Comma Press), was described by the Guardian as 'muscular and memorable'. More at www.michellegreen.co.uk

Miki Byrne has had three collections of poetry published, and work included in over 170 respected poetry magazines/anthologies. She has won poetry competitions, been placed in others, and read on both radio and TV. She has also judged poetry competitions and was a finalist for Gloucester Poet Laureate. Miki contributes to Poems in the Waiting Room, and sometimes writes for *Arthritis Care* magazine. She began reading her work in a bikers' club.

Miss Jacqui is a spoken word artist, mix engineer, facilitator and artist manager. Her love for spoken word/poetry came to light in 2011, when she joined 'Poets Platform' led by Kat Francois. Since then she has performed at various events including the Paralympic Team Welcoming and Opening ceremonies. Miss Jacqui has worked with Halfmoon Young Peoples Theatre, Theatre Royal Stratford East, National Youth Theatre and Channel 4 News. She is also the youngest board member of Graeae. Twitter: @iAmMissJacqui

'Stare' was performed live by Miss Jacqui and filmed by Leonore

Schick at Sisters of Frida: Disabled Women's Voices from the Frontline, Blackfriars Settlement (London), 9 July 2016 – and is part of the online extension of this book.

Naomi Woddis is a writer and photographer. She has presented work at the London Literature Festival, Southbank Centre, Courtauld Institute of Art, National Gallery, O2 Wireless Festival and Theatre Royal Stratford East. Her photography has been exhibited at Ovalhouse, The Albany, Lewisham Art House, The Nunnery Gallery and The Pie Factory, Margate. She is particularly interested in online participatory projects and the links that can be made between image and text.

'Impregnate' uses Terrance Hayes' technique, 'A gram of &s'; the last word of each line is a word found in the title.

Nuala Watt lives in Glasgow. She has cerebral palsy, a visual impairment and epilepsy. She recently completed a PhD from the University of Glasgow on the poetics of partial sight. Her poems have appeared in *Magma* and *Gutter,* as well as on BBC Radio 3 and in a recent anthology of new Scottish poetry *Be The First To Like This* (Vagabond Voices, 2014.) In 2015 she received a John Mather Charitable Trust bursary from the Scottish Poetry Library.

'On Her Partial Blindness', 'The View', 'Receiving My Poems in Braille' and 'Evangelist' were originally published in a pamphlet from Calderwood Press. 'On Her Partial Blindness' has also been published in The Scotsman and in *Anthology of Scottish Poets* (Bibliotheca Universalis, 2016: eds. Evans and Leadbetter).

Rachael Boast was born in Suffolk in 1975. *Sidereal* (Picador 2011) won the Forward Prize for Best First Collection, and the Seamus Heaney Centre for Poetry Prize. She is co-editor of *The Echoing Gallery: Bristol Poets and Art in the City* (Redcliffe Press). *Pilgrim's Flower* (Picador, 2013) was shortlisted for the Griffin Prize. *Void Studies* (Picador, 2016) was shortlisted for the T.S. Eliot Prize. Rachael lives in Bristol.

'Aubade' was originally published in *Pilgrim's Flower*.

Raisa Kabir is a South Asian Queer Crip Femme (of Colour). She is a cultural activist, writer and artist. She uses contemporary textiles and photography to interrogate and question concepts around the politics of dress and space, in connection to the queer brown gendered body. She has written about South Asian queer dress, identity and culture, queer femme of colour invisibility, as well as cultural appropriation, ethnicity, diaspora and dress.

Raymond Antrobus Raymond Antrobus is a Jamaican British poet, performer and hearing aid user, born and bred in Hackney, East London. His poems have been published in magazines and literary journals such as *The Rialto, Magma, Oxford Diaspora's Programme, British Council Literature, Shooter Literary Journal, The Missing Slate, Morning Star* and *Media Diversified,* and are forthcoming in *Wasafiri* and Bloodaxe's *Ten.* Raymond has read and performed at festivals (Glastonbury, Latitude, etc.) and universities (including Oxford, Goldsmiths and Warwick).

'What Is Possible' was first published by *The Rialto* and appeared in Raymond's pamphlet, *To Sweeten Bitten* (Outspoken Press). 'Dear Hearing World' was originally published in *Deaf Poets Society:* an online journal of deaf and disabled literature & art.

Rosamund McCullain: Originally from West Yorkshire, I came to Mid Wales in 1983 to study English at Aberystwyth University. I have been writing for many years for my own pleasure and sanity. I write mainly poetry but some prose. I wrote a short novel, *The Dispossessed*, about mental health issues and the mental health system (published by Chipmunka, 2005).

Rose Cook is an Apples & Snakes poet, and has appeared at many of their events. Rose co-founded the popular Devon poetry and performance forum, One Night Stanza, as well as the poetry performance group, Dangerous Cardigans. Her latest book, *Notes From a Bright Field*, was published by Cultured Llama in 2013. Previous poetry books are *everyday festival* (HappenStance Press, 2009) and *Taking Flight* (Oversteps Books, 2009).

'The Chalice and The Heart' was previously published in 'The Broadsheet 2014'.

Sandra Alland is a writer, interdisciplinary artist and curator whose poetry collections include *Blissful Times* (BookThug, 2007) and *Naturally Speaking* (espresso, 2012). Sandra also publishes with Comma Press and Disability Arts Online, and curates Scotland's Cachín Cachán Cachunga! Queer & Trans Cabaret. Interests: engineering strange performance hybrids; promoting queer, trans, working class, racialised, D/deaf and/or disabled artists; collaborating with other crips; dreaming up artistically-integrated access; foiling the upper classes' plans of domination. www.blissfultimes.ca

'Unparalleled poetic assistance into the Canon UK' was written in collaboration with Dragon NaturallySpeaking voice dictation software. 'The Unforgotten, or Mary do you want to talk about last night' features an x-ray of San's spine, and is a cut-up of found text from the television and San's poetry.

Saradha Soobrayen studied Live Art, Visual Art and Creative Writing. Her critical texts, fiction and poems are widely published. She received an Eric Gregory Award in 2004 and the Pacuare Nature Reserve Laureateship in 2015. She works as a poetry editor and writing mentor, and as a Poetry Library assistant. Her latest project is a poetic inquiry into the depopulation of the Chagos Archipelago: a melange of political rhetoric, poetic methodology, Kreol and song lyrics. www. saradhasoobrayen.com

'Their homecoming is not yet out of reach, not yet out of sight' and 'I will arise and go now, and go to Innisfree, and build a small cabin...' were previously published in *Long Poem Magazine, Dodos and Dragons 2* and *Pacuare Poems 2015*.

Sarah Golightley is an Edinburgh-based mental health researcher with an interest in the emerging discipline of Mad Studies. She lives and writes about the interlocking of mental health distress, chronic illness, and physical dis/abilities. She has created several zines on mental health, sexuality and gender. She's keen on creating alternative and critical thought on inclusion, queerness, dis/ability and capitalism.

sean burn is a writer, performer and self-taught artist with an international reputation and active involvement in disability arts. seán is part of north-east mad studies collective. his last full volume of poetry, *is that a bruise or a tattoo?*, is still available from shearsman press. http://www.shearsman.com/ws-shop/category/841-burn-sean/product/4355-sean-burn-is-that-a-bruise-or-a-tattoo

'Untitled' is from the sequence, 'tattooing lorca', originally published in *wings are giving out* (skrev press, 2009).

Stephanie Conn is a former teacher, a graduate of the MA programme at the Seamus Heaney Centre, Belfast, and a recipient of an Arts Council Career Enhancement Award. Her debut collection, *The Woman on the Other Side*, was published by Doire Press last year. Her pamphlet, *Copeland's Daughter*, won the Poetry Business 2016 Competition and is published by Smith/Doorstep.

'Mercury' and 'View from a Rocking Chair' were first published in *The Woman on the Other Side* (Doire Press, 2016).

Thank Yous

Special thanks:

Many writers submitted to *Stairs and Whispers* through connection with Markie Burnhope. Markie was originally one of our editors, but had to step down for health reasons. We thank her for her immense help in laying the groundwork – this book wouldn't have happened without her.

Daniel Sluman thanks:

A massive thank you to my co-editors, for not only giving me the best editorial experience I could imagine, but also for giving me the blueprint for the level of empathy, understanding, and professional support I will put forward and expect in return in any further collaborative projects I'm involved with. Also, to the contributors, for helping form such a strong and diverse body of work, and for educating me with a new understanding of many disabilities and illnesses, and how they intersect with gender, race, sexual identity, and class. Jane Commane deserves the biggest thank you for seeing the merit in this project, and backing it through the wonderful Nine Arches Press, and I need to also give a big shout out to my family, especially my father, and my wife, for helping me during this project's development.

Khairani Barokka thanks:

My great thanks to Sandra Alland and Daniel Sluman for brilliant comradeship, Jane Commane, Markie Burnhope, my loved ones, and everyone who submitted to this anthology. I'm grateful to have worked on a project that feels so right as a way to open up conversations, emotions and hopefully, community. I dedicate my work here to everyone in such communities who has ever made me feel welcome.

Sandra Alland thanks:

Okka and Daniel, for being the best co-conspirators a crip could dream of (of which a crip could dream harhar). Jane Commane and Nine Arches Press, for transforming this ambitious project from dream into reality. All the contributors for their brilliant work. All who submitted and spread the word. Ania Urhanowska, for serious skills with a camera and computer. K. Yvonne Strain, for BSL interpreting and translation consultation. Donna Williams, Alison Smith, EJ Raymond, Danni Wright, Turtléar and Jenny Sealey, for BSL translations and video support on creating accessible information. AB Silvera, for captioning assistance and skills with shadows. Sophie Mayer and Markie Burnhope, you know why. My international crip family, for keeping me afloat. Matson Lawrence, for everything.

Nine Arches Press thanks:

Huge gratitude and thanks are due to all those who have been editors of this anthology – Sandra, Dan, Khairani, and Markie – for their creation, development and direction of this anthology. Their work on this book has been phenomenal. Without their belief, energy and dedication to the project, it simply could never have happened.

Thanks are due to all the poets for each contribution they made to this anthology, and also for their time in contributing audio recordings and films to help make this book both multi-media and accessible. Thank you also to the film-makers, BSL interpreters, assistants and many others who played a vital role in helping this project to come together. Thanks are also due to Writing West Midlands, Gregory Leadbetter and the Institute of Creative and Critical Writing at Birmingham City University for their continued support of this project.

Our Supporters

This project was supported and made possible by funding from Arts Council England through Grants for the Arts, and by crowdfunding through Crowdfunder.

Many thanks are due to these individual crowdfunding sponsors for their encouragement, generosity and support for *Stairs and Whispers*:

Abegail Morley
Alan Baker
Alexander Herbert
Alison Brackenbury
Amy Claridge
Amy Key
Amy Mackelden
Andrea Davis
Andrew Fentham
Andy Eycott
Aneeqa
Angeline
Anna Beddow
Ann-Marie McManaman
Anonymous
Anthea Simmons
Asim Khan
Bare Fiction
Bekah Hughes
Bernard Kelly
Bohdan Piasecki
Bookartbookshop
Brian Lavelle
Calum Gardner

Caroline Smith
Catherine Ingram Smith
Charles Coventry
Chloe Smith
Chrissy Williams
Claire Askew
Claire Trevien
CN Lester
Colin Herd
Corrie Hodgson & Beth Mills
Cynthia Miller
D Franklin
Dave Coates
David Clarke
David Hirons
David Turner
David Varley
Deborah Alma
Deryn Rees-Jones
Ed Doegar
Elly Nobbs
Emily Berry
Emma Geen
Emma Lee

Fiona Benson
Fiona Moore
Freya Gosnold
Geraldine Clarkson
Gwyneth Terrell
Hannah Hodgson
Hilda Sheehan
Isobel Dixon
J V Birch
Jacqueline Saphra
Janet Hatherley
Janet Vaughan
Jean Hockley
Jenna Clake
Jenny Fowler
Jessica Mookherjee
Jesus Canduela
Jo Bell
Jo Weston
Jonathan Davidson
Joseph Frances
Julia Watts Belser
K Brook
Kaite O'Reilly
Kate Wakeling
Katherine McMahon
Kathryn Maris
Katie Griffiths
Katy Hastie
Kay Syrad
Kirsten Irving
KM Augustine
Lauren Mulholland
Lawrence Schimel

Leo Yannick Wild
Lindsay Macgregor
Liz Berry
Liz Munro
Lou Sarabadzic
Louisa Campbell
Luise Kocaurek
Luke Kennard
Marianthi Makra
Mat Riches
Mathew Lyons
Maxine Smith
Mel Pryor
Morris Berg
Nancy Mattson
Naomi Nu McAdam
Natalie Wright
Nathalie Teitler
Nellie Cole
Nuala Watt
Paige Kimble
Pam Thompson
Pearl Pirie
Penny Montague
Peter J. King
Peter Raynard
Pey Colborne
Philip Hood
Pippery
Rachael Nicholas
Rachel Mann
Rebecca Durham
Rebecca Jones
Richard Vaughan

Rishi Dastidar

Robert Peake

Rosa

Rosamund Taylor

Rowena Knight

Roy Mcfarlane

Roz Goddard

Ruby Robinson

Sally Vince

Samantha Bennett

Sara Rhys-Martin

Sarah Leavesley

Shaun Lawrence

Simon Cole-Hamilton

Sophie Fenella

Stephanie Conn

Stephen Daniels

Steve Venright

Steven

Stuart Bartholomew

Sue Finch

Suzannah Evans

Suzanne Kavanagh

Tamar Yoseloff

Tania Carlisle

Tania Hershman

Wasi Daniju

Wendy Tuxworth

William Gallagher

Yevgeny Salisbury

Zeba Talkhani